WALTER GROPIUS

D1608605

THE MASTERS OF
WORLD ARCHITECTURE SERIES

UNDER THE GENERAL EDITORSHIP OF WILLIAM ALEX

ALVAR AALTO by Frederick Gutheim
LE CORBUSIER by Françoise Choay
ANTONIO GAUDÍ by George R. Collins
WALTER GROPIUS by James M. Fitch
ERIC MENDELSOHN by Wolf Von Eckardt
LUDWIG MIES VAN DER ROHE by Arthur Drexler
PIER LUIGI NERVI by Ada Louise Huxtable
RICHARD NEUTRA by Esther McCoy
OSCAR NIEMEYER by Stamo Papadaki
LOUIS SULLIVAN by Albert Bush-Brown
FRANK LLOYD WRIGHT by Vincent Scully, Jr.

walter gropius

by James Marston Fitch

DISTRIBUTED BY POCKET BOOKS, INC.

George Braziller, Inc.
NEW YORK, 1960

CONTENTS

Text   7

   1. Gropius, the Educator   10

   2. Gropius, the Architect and Designer   18

   3. Gropius, the Social Critic   28

Plates   33

Notes to the Text   113

Selected Chronological List of Buildings and Projects   115

Chronology   117

Selected Bibliography of Books and Articles

  by Walter Gropius   120

Selected Bibliography on Walter Gropius   122

Index   124

Sources of Illustrations   128

THE SHAKERS AND MAKERS of the modern world—such figures as Einstein, Shaw, Matisse or Wright—all spent their lives under a very special set of historical conditions. They lived to be very old men in a period of fantastically accelerated social change. Unlike the great prophets of past times, they survived not merely to see their predictions come true: they lived on into a world in which their works had become commonplace, the very warp and woof of everyday life. The prophet had overrun his prophecy.

This situation, so novel in human affairs, has created a dilemma both for them and for us who have so hugely profited from their efforts. It means that they have existed for us at two distinctly different levels: they have simultaneously the scale of legendary heroes and the normal dimensions of colleagues and contemporaries. And this has complicated enormously the necessary task of weighing their contributions to contemporary life.

Walter Gropius, at the age of 77, confronts us with just such a dilemma. One of the few actual inventors of modern architecture, the creator of the world famous *Bauhaus* and the most influential architectural teacher alive, Gropius is, at the same time, a successful practicing architect with the greatest volume of work in his entire career. He is an active and vocal member of a profession which has been powerfully shaped by standards which he himself helped establish, many years ago, in another land. The profession itself has hundreds of his pupils, hundreds of admirers and thousands of others who, whether they know it or not, have been affected by his example. Gropius thus moves in a world which is doubly of his making: made by him then and made again today.

Throughout a long and active life in international architecture, he has played three interconnected yet separate roles: designer, educator, and critic. His contributions in all three areas have been impressive, though they have fluctuated in relative importance from decade to decade. The disasters of modern history have played a large role in this fluctuation, sharply dividing his life into several distinct phases.

This life began on May 18, 1883, when he was born into the family of a Berlin architect, Walter Gropius and his wife Manon. He received an architectural education in the Universities of Charlottenburg and Munich in the first years of the 20th century. But this education was interrupted, first, by a trip to Spain (1904–05), where he toured the country and worked in a ceramic factory; and secondly by the usual stint in the Imperial Army (1905–06). His life as an architect really began when he entered the office of Germany's most famous architect, Peter Behrens, as an apprentice: he stayed there three years (1907–10) to become Behrens' chief assistant. He could not have chosen a happier point of beginning, for Behrens stood in much the same relation to modern German architecture as did Louis Sullivan to American. The Behrens office was a magnet which attracted many bright young men—how strong a magnet may be deduced from the fact that Walter Gropius, Ludwig Mies (later van der Rohe) and Charles Jeanneret (later Le Corbusier) were all three employed there!

Gropius himself, with his usual meticulous candor, says of Behrens: "I owe him much, particularly the habit of thinking in principles . . . an imposing personality, well-dressed and having the cool deportment of a conservative Hamburg patrician, [he was] endowed with will power and a penetrating intellect . . . moved more by reason than emotion."[1] Gropius also owed the Behrens office his first contact with modern industry; for Behrens, in his capacity as design consultant to the German electrical trust, was perhaps the first architect in history to hold this essentially modern post. Through this contact, Gropius was exposed to the whole range of design problems from that of the factory down to the products manufactured there.

From 1910, when he left the Behrens office, to 1914, Gropius was a brilliant young architect in practice for himself: this phase was brutally truncated by the four-year hiatus of World War I. From 1919 through 1928, he functioned primarily as an educator. Then he resumed practice in Berlin, where he remained until 1934, when he fled Nazi Germany—first to London, where he was an architect for three years; then to Harvard in 1937, there to be an educator again for fifteen years. Since his retirement in 1952, he has again become a full-time practicing architect.

This is, as we shall see, a schematic account of a complex and fully-rounded life, for Gropius has never ceased to be active at every level of his chosen field. He has always been an outspoken critic and consistent theoretician of the social aspects of architecture, housing and city planning. This criticism was perhaps most trenchant (as it was probably most comprehensive) during the German years (1919–34); but his recent statements show that there has been no diminution in his social convictions. He has been a continuously influential architect. It was as the designer of two sensational buildings that his career began; his middle years were marked by immensely significant projects, including those for the Bauhaus itself; and it is as the architect of the great new University of Bagdad that his career is now being capped. But these two aspects of his career, important as they have been, are not the center of his fame and influence. The lever with which Gropius moved the world was a design of another order: a great educational invention, the school of the *Bauhaus*.

1. GROPIUS, THE EDUCATOR

THE REVOLUTION WHICH he began that April day in 1919 when he created the Bauhaus was to set off a widening circle of repercussions which would ultimately leave not a corner of the globe untouched. Who would have guessed, when he signed the contract with "the Court Chamberlain's Office, acting with the consent of the Provisional Republican Government of Saxe-Weimar"[2] (the very ambiguity of the phrasing reflects the political revolution which was rocking Germany)— who would have guessed that theories were being evolved which would one day shape buildings and artifacts, fabrics and furniture, in the islands of Japan, the coasts of Brazil, the steaming valley of the Tigris? And how could that young German architect have guessed that these same theories would guide him, decades later, in the design of buildings in (of all improbable places!) Athens and Bagdad for (of all unlikely clients!) the United States Government and the King of Iraq.[3] How elliptical is history!

Young American architects who have reached maturity since World War II are often no more aware of the historic significance of the Bauhaus than a young jet pilot would be of the Wright Brothers' work at Kitty Hawk. So it is possible, in such circles, either to hear this significance denied or else to have the Bauhaus blamed for all sorts of disasters which have subsequently overtaken design. Yet Gropius himself could say in 1960 that, had he his life as an educator to live over, he would feel it necessary to change his theories "only in detail."[4] There is no arrogance here: this is the sober conviction of a modest man. Whose estimate, then, is correct? Whose judgment corresponds most closely to objective reality?

If we analyze the ideological positions which Gropius staked out for the Bauhaus at its very inception, and if we study the body of work which grew out of it in the following decade, then we can only conclude that these principles were neither mistaken in 1919 nor obsolete in 1960. For a central aspect of his work in education has been his understanding of the dangers to design inherent in the separation of head and hand, theory and practice, intellectual and manual worker, artist and craftsman. He has tried always to bridge the arbitrary divisions between the two, to reunite them for the common enrichment of both. The Staatliches Bauhaus in Weimar offered the first and most comprehensive opportunity he had to put his theories into practice. Even the two existing schools which he merged to form the new institution symbolize this ambition: the Grand Ducal School of Applied Arts and the Grand Ducal Academy of Arts. The curriculum which he devised for this combination was a rational effort to merge the best of craft training with all that was valid in the academy. He was opposed to "art for art's sake," believing that every artist was first of all a craftsman: "only in rare blessed moments of inspiration, moments beyond the control of his will, his work may blossom into art."[5] Thus every Bauhaus student—no matter what his ambitions or abilities—went through the same workshop training. At the same time, Gropius was careful never to vulgarize the distinction between competence and creativity:

> Art, in fact, is not a branch of science which can be learned step by step, from a book. Innate artistic ability can [not be taught but] only intensified by influencing the whole being . . . the ability to draw is all too frequently confused with the ability to produce creative design. Like dexterity in handicrafts, it is, however, no more than a skill . . . virtuosity . . . is not art.[6]

He aimed at avoiding both the boorish illiteracy of the modern craftsman and the irresponsible precocity of the academically trained artist. Thus he hoped to re-create in the world of modern industrial society the same sort of healthy, organic unity in all phases of design that had characterized all pre-industrial societies.

It is a measure of his maturity (as well as that of his circle generally) that Gropius was able to steer an even course between those extremes on which so many theories foundered. The specific principles upon which the Bauhaus was founded are not easily encapsulated. Gropius himself found it necessary to amplify and develop them repeatedly after the publication of the first manifesto[7] but in essence they were these:

1. "The Bauhaus believes the machine to be our modern medium of design and seeks to come to terms with it."[8]
2. All design must recognize this fact of life and distill a new set of esthetic criteria from it. Such a process would, for architecture, lead to "clear, organic [form] whose inner logic will be radiant and naked, unencumbered by lying façades and trickeries."[9]

3. The Bauhaus teaches "the common citizenship of all forms of creative work and their logical interdependence upon one another."[10]
4. The scale and complexity of modern problems necessitates collaborative design. "Any industrially produced object is the result of countless experiments, of long systematic research."[11] The design school must recognize this and equip the student with "the common basis on which many individuals are able to create together a superior unit of work."[12]
5. The education of the designer "must include a thorough, practical manual training in workshops actively engaged in production, coupled with sound theoretical instruction in the laws of design."[13]

This was the program which catapulted the Bauhaus into international prominence, making it the most important single force in the design world in the period between the wars. Every field of design registered its influence: architecture, product design, furniture; fabrics, silverware and pottery; graphics, typography, painting, advertising; photography, movies, stagecraft, even ballet. And everywhere its influence was benign. As a program, its capacity to regenerate design derived from its essentially correct analysis of the relation between design and production in an industrialized world.

In its short and crisis-ridden life, the Bauhaus trained over 500 men and women in various fields. Its publications, exhibitions and lectures so precisely filled a vacuum that its influence was out of all proportion to its size. It irradiated all of Western Europe and—after Gropius' arrival at Harvard in 1937—America. Though the Bauhaus curriculum could not be applied at the Graduate School of Design, the Gropius philosophy of design could.[14] It made Harvard into a leading world center of architectural studies and produced a whole generation of designers who have now emerged as leaders of the profession. The durability of the Bauhaus concept is proved by the fact that designers have been coasting for decades upon the momentum generated by those first historic years at Weimar and Dessau. Yet education for design has not followed the precedent set by the Bauhaus: it seems instead to have taken the opposite path. Art schools and trade schools have proliferated; but where in the world today is there an institution which faces the problem as squarely, as profoundly, as did the Bauhaus in its time?

Or is this program obsolete, as many contemporary critics today maintain? Does an analysis of objective conditions reveal any fundamental change which would make it less valuable? The fact is that the conditions against which Gropius reacted in 1919 have grown steadily more acute in the western world and most acute of all in America. Industrial production grows continuously more complex, dominating every aspect of life. The designer is more and more removed from any control over, or any real understanding of, science and technology. And the process of design deteriorates into mere cosmetics: robbed of any firm base of function, it has become the prisoner of fad and fashion. In such a context it should be clear that, far from having "outgrown" the need for a Bauhaus-type education, we need it more than ever.

Two charges, both of them esthetic, are brought against the Bauhaus by its critics today. The first is that it established a *style;* the second is that that style is "bad." These charges, though related, are not at all the same thing. Gropius has always denied that he had any ambition to establish a *style;* he has always maintained that, on the contrary, it was a basic *methodology* of design which he sought. In his very first statement on arriving in this country in 1937 he said:

> It is not my intention to introduce a . . . cut and dried "Modern Style" from Europe, but rather to introduce a method of approach which allows one to tackle a problem according to its peculiar conditions . . . an attitude toward the problems of our generation which is unbiased, original and elastic.[15]

A democrat at heart and a tireless advocate of collaborative work, he has repeatedly rejected what seemed to him to be the dictatorial implications in the issue of style. When a sapling was planted in Chicago in honor of his 70th birthday, he said he hoped it would grow into "a tree in which birds of many colors and shapes [could] sit and feel sustained. . . . I realize that I am a figure covered with many labels . . . "Bauhaus Style," "International Style," "Functional Style"—these have almost succeeded in hiding the human core behind it all." And he was eager, he went on, to escape this caricature of his real position.[16] There is something at once comic and sad in the repeated efforts of this great man to disentangle himself from a semantic snare which is of no real consequence anyway. For whenever any group of men agree upon a common method of accomplishing common tasks, a common system of expression (i.e., a style) will ultimately appear. Ours is the first period in history to be embarrassed by this cultural certainty.

Gropius has himself become the victim of industrialism's fantastic capacity for mimicry and multiplication. A powerful designer, committed to a "suprapersonal" style of expression, he has always attracted students and disciples; and as his fame and influence spread, he was paid the compliment of piracy and parody of what he designed. The same thing happened to the Bauhaus. It furnished the world with a new set of prototypes; too often the world merely made them into stereotypes. A third of a century later these prototypes may very well be inadequate for today's tastes and sensibilities. But this does not alter the fact that the Bauhaus, in its day, was not the jailor but the liberator of the Western designer, giving him the first stylistic freedom he had enjoyed since the end of the Medieval period.

The other charge against the Bauhaus runs thus: it created a style which was "bad" because it was "cold," "inhuman," "narrowly functional," "mechanistic," etc. These are the judgments of a generation which took no part in the great esthetic battles of the Twenties and which is consequently in no position to understand the terms of that revolutionary struggle. The only way that modern form could evolve from the *fin de siècle* morass was to disavow *all* the past: here the artistic revolution paralleled the political. Evaluations must take account of this historic fact. The fight was very bitter, with no quarter asked or given and opinion polarized around extreme positions. After all, for "purely" esthetic reasons, the Bauhaus was twice driven out of its home (by reactionaries in Weimar in 1925; by the Nazis in Dessau in 1932.) It was denounced as "art-bolshevism which must be wiped out": storm troopers called on the "national German Spirit" to "rescue" German art from the modernists[17]—a task which Hitler was shortly to accomplish with gruesome thoroughness.

There was no shortage of wit, passion or courage among the partisans of the new architecture: here Gropius was neither first nor alone. Already before World War I, the Viennese architect Adolf Loos had penned a wickedly effective attack on historic ornament (and, by extension, on eclecticism in general). In his famous essay, *Ornament and Crime,* he wrote: "The artist used to stand for health and strength, at the pinnacle of humanity; but the modern ornamentalist is either a cultural laggard or a pathological case." Loos argued that no ornament at all was permissible to civilized man: the Papuans, since they were aborigines, might be forgiven if they "tattoo their skins, decorate their boats, their oars—everything they can get their hands on. But a modern man who tattoos himself . . . [is] either a latent criminal or a degenerate aristocrat . . . The true greatness of our age [is] that it can no longer bring forth ornament. We have vanquished ornament," Loos boasted, "and broken through into an ornamentless world . . . Freedom from ornament is a sign of mental strength."[18]

Gropius himself, in the first spring of peace, had written a fiery call for that new "radiant and naked" architecture:

> Is not [architecture] the crystallized expression of the noblest thoughts of man, his ardor, his humanity, his faith, his religion? All this it used to be—once. But who, in our period of accursed expediency, lets himself still be enraptured by its all-embracing message? We should cry out in shame against these wastes of ugliness when walking through our streets

and cities! Let us face it! These drab, hollow and meaningless fakeries in which we live and work will leave behind a mortifying testimony to the spiritual fall from grace of our generation.

And then the call to the esthetic barricades:

> Artists, architects, let us remove the barriers between the arts which a perverted academic training has erected . . . Together, let us will, conceive, create a new architecture! . . . here is our hope: that the power of the idea, a growing vision of a courageous, far-reaching new conception of the art of architecture will imbue the builders of a more fortunate future which is bound to come.[19]

It was in terms such as these that the battle was fought. The furnace of controversy burned up the sweet, the pretty, the soft, with all their connotations of decadence. The new forms were to be pure, cool and abstract—ventilated by justice, lighted by reason. How far the blazing passions of World War I had driven the generation which fought it is dramatized in the first show of the young (and wounded) veteran from the Eastern front, Moholy-Nagy. In 1922, in a gallery called *Der Sturm,* he exhibited a number of Constructivist canvases, including three which had been painted by telephone! "He dictated the paintings to the foreman in a sign factory," his widow wrote, "using a color chart and an order blank of graph paper to specify the location of form elements and their exact hue."[20] Here was the ultimate effort to purify art of all human passion, to lift it above the personal, the subjective, the fallible and to establish the objective independence of visual form, divorced from all narrative.

Much of this work aspired to be "functional"—i.e., to extract its formal properties directly from the task to be performed: surely that ambition needs no apology or defense. It is also true that, simultaneously, much of this new form drew its inspiration directly from the machine. Science and technology appeared to that generation as much safer paragons than human passion. Here again Moholy defines its attitude, this time verbally, in one of those incandescent manifestoes which were so usual at the time:

> The reality of our century is technology: the invention, construction and maintenance of the machine. To be a user of the machine is to be of the spirit of this century. It has replaced the transcendental spiritualism of past eras . . .

And from this he draws what seemed to the period the necessary conclusions:

> This is the root of Socialism, the final liquidation of feudalism . . .
> Make your peace with it.[21]

Most of the great figures of the period shared this general perspective—poems, paintings, sculptures, ballet, sonata, and cinema all celebrated the forms, movements, and promises of the machine. Thus, when Le Corbusier's famous dictum ("the house a machine for living") echoed Gropius' ("we want an architecture adapted to our world of machines") both were speaking the very language of Western humanism in the early 1920's.

Yet, even in those enthusiastic years, Gropius was no blindly uncritical worshiper of technology. "Mechanized work is lifeless, proper only to the lifeless machine," he warned. "So long as the machine-economy remains an end in itself, rather than a means of freeing the intellect from the burden of mechanized labor, the individual will remain enslaved and society will remain disordered."[22] He aspired to the mastery of the machine by the designer to create a serene and anonymous architecture, capable of flexible response to the demands of life upon it. And this conscious effort at purification is precisely what has given the idiom of Gropius and his colleagues at the Bauhaus its amazing durability. Time has its own special method of isolating the meretricious and ephemeral in art and of exposing it to the merciless ridicule of simple distance. In this context, the Bauhaus record is admirable: few objects from that period have survived as well as Gropius' Tribune Tower of 1922 (plate 11) or Adler automobile of 1930 (plate 52). And Paul Klee's paintings, Marcel Breuer's chairs, Anni Albers' textiles, continue to display that stylistic durability which is internal evidence of continuing validity.

The diffidence of modern artists and architects before the very word *style* is understandable. It has its origins precisely in the Bauhaus period and is the result of their traumatic experience—in what Hitchcock once called the dark night of eclecticism—in being forced to employ dead styles to express living artistic concepts. (We would have a roughly comparable situation today if we compelled the nuclear physicist to express his concepts of the universe in the English of Beowulf or the French of Abbé Suger.) And yet, if the revolt against the historic styles became by extension the rejection of style itself, the results would be visually anarchic as well as intellectually absurd. Gropius has always been aware of this paradox. On the one hand, he has correctly argued that "the creation of standard types for everyday use is a social necessity." And for him the search for that standard "implies the seeking out of the best, the separation of the essential and suprapersonal from the personal and accidental." The standard thus becomes "a cultural title of honor."[23] At the same time, as he elsewhere recognizes, the "successive repetition of an expression which has become settled already as a common denominator for a whole period" is just what constitutes a style! Nevertheless, great danger lies in

> . . . the attempt to classify and thereby to freeze living art and architecture, while it is still in the formative stage, into a "style" or "ism." [This] is more likely to stifle than to stimulate creative activity.[24]

The distinction, while it may seem subtle, has always seemed to him extremely important and he has returned to it again only recently:

> Neither I nor my many collaborators at the Bauhaus had the idea of reaching a "style." My notion was to avoid the usual teaching in art schools where the director or teacher produces small editions of himself. We sought to find a method of approach for giving the student objective findings related to our way of seeing and experiencing physical and psychological facts. This is very different from consciously working toward a "style." Of course, it is clear that the historian, in looking backwards, will perceive a certain style expression of the Bauhaus.[25]

His distrust of premature verbalization leads him to a characteristic position:

> Styles in my opinion should be named and outlined by the historian only for past periods. In the present we lack the dispassionate attitude necessary for impersonal judgment of what is going on. As humans, we are vain and jealous and that distorts objective vision. Why don't we leave it, then, to the future historian to settle the history of today's growth in architecture—and get to work and let grow?[26]

We can accept his advice, provided that we realize that everything we do, by the very manner of our doing it, will enable future historians to identify us by our stylistic characteristics as easily as we can, today, be identified by our fingerprints.

2. GROPIUS, THE ARCHITECT AND DESIGNER

ONE MIGHT ALMOST say of the whole corpus of his work that, over half a century, it shows very little development: but this is merely an oblique way of saying that half a century's perspective shows it to have been almost completely developed and mature at its very birth. Stylistically, Gropius leapt into maturity at an early age and with scarcely any fumbling. Simple truth, therefore, entitles him to say "I had already found my ground in architecture before the First World War, as is evidenced in the Fagus Building and the Cologne Werkbund Exhibition in 1914."[27] Part of this phenomenal maturity is due to Gropius and part to the intellectual environment in which he matured.

When he opened his own office in 1910, the world had been prepared for him by at least a generation of searching architects. On both sides of the Atlantic, the revolt against 19th-century eclecticism was being fought, to disestablish the dictatorship of historic styles and to create a new, fresh idiom derived from modern needs, employing modern materials and techniques, and expressing modern aspirations. The actual point of contact with this struggle came to Gropius through his apprenticeship to Peter Behrens (1868–1940). Behrens himself had studied with the great Viennese pioneer, Otto Wagner, and had thus profited from the most cosmopolitan *ambiente* of Europe. But many other innovators of Behrens' generation had prepared the way for Gropius: Joseph Hoffman and Adolf Loos, the Viennese; the Belgians H. P. Berlage, Victor Horta and Henry van de Velde—the latter Gropius' immediate predecessor at Weimar; the Spaniard Antonio Gaudí; the Britishers C. F. A. Voysey and Charles Rennie MacIntosh; and finally the Americans Louis Sullivan and Frank Lloyd Wright. All of these men had attacked the central problem, their perspectives modified by national conditions and personal propensities.

The result was a whole spectrum of stylistic movements (Secessionstil, Art Nouveau, Jugendstil, Modernismo, Chicago School) as well as some highly personal idioms such as those of Gaudí and Wright. So many countercurrents were bound to be confusing to the younger generation; it is the more remarkable how little they confused Gropius, how completely he seems to have digested all these stimuli by the time he did his first building in 1911. (Digested is the proper word because— already well-educated, well-traveled and widely read—he would have been thoroughly familiar with them all.) Yet the Fagus factory is an unmistakably original building, with nothing derivative about it.

Looking back at this factory across half a century, we are apt to miss its significance for the simple reason that it seems so familiar. That separation of building tissue into skeleton and skin which it celebrated so dramatically is a commonplace nowadays: the world is full of glass and metal curtain walls hung outside a steel or concrete frame. Yet the Fagus building is the first to extract the full esthetically revolutionary impact from this structural development (plate 1). Gropius, of course, was not the first to use it: there were dozens of American skyscrapers which already employed it; and in point of fact, his Fagus structure was actually a hybrid construction of brick columns, steel beams and concrete floor-slabs and stairways. Yet artistically the Fagus plant is a much clearer statement than many structurally "pure" skyscrapers. For by reducing his wall to a transparent screen of glass and metal and then hanging it *outside* the columns, he made its nonstructural function brilliantly explicit. Then by moving the corner column back from its historic location, cantilevering out the unsupported floor slab and enclosing this open corner with a glass screen, he was able to dramatize the skeletal lightness and grace of the whole system.

It seems quite safe to say that, esthetically, this combination is a Gropius invention. Though Behrens used the steel skeleton, he effectively concealed the fact by sheathing it in seemingly load-bearing brick walls: in the Berlin Turbine Factory of 1909 (plate 1a), the corners are enclosed in mammoth brick corner piers which flatly contradict the steel frame behind. Gropius might well have seen the way Wright's ribbon windows gave transparency to the corners of his Prairie houses. (Wright had been published in Germany the year before.) But in both the multistory Larkin Building of 1904 (plate 1b) and the monumental Unity Temple of 1906 Wright had used massive corner pylons to dramatize the cubist solidity of his forms: they are the very antithesis of the skeletal. Even Sullivan's elegant skeletal expression in the Schlesinger-Meyer Store (1899) misses part of the problem by giving equal weight to column and spandrel and then recessing the glass in deep reveals: the result is still a wall with windows, not a curtain wall (plate 1c). Gropius, in the Fagus Building, has given us something qualitatively new—a manner of expressing the skeletal structure that was to become a constituent fact, as Giedion would put it, of contemporary architecture.

The difference between Gropius and the older men under whose influence and tutelage he had matured is even clearer three years later in the great Werkbund Exhibition at Cologne. Here were Behrens with his Exhibition Hall; van de Velde with his Theater; Hoffman with his Austrian Pavilion. One has only to contrast these buildings with Gropius' model factory to see how far the younger man had progressed beyond the great pioneers. The building is notable on several counts. It displays his absolute freedom from any dependence upon historic form (a dependence embarrassingly evident in the skim-milk classicism of Hoffman's Pavilion). And it shows how he had freed himself of any tinge of ornamentalism (a tendency all too apparent in the sickly-sweet curves which van de Velde imposed on his Theater). Indeed, Gropius' forms have such a pristine newness and contemporaneity that they might almost be laid to a blessed ignorance of the past. Since we know that he was not ignorant of the beguiling alternatives of eclecticism, we can only conclude that he had completely freed himself of their grasp. Gropius, in other words, is not a transitional figure: his work lies wholly on this side of the great divide of the modern movement.

The Werkbund complex has—to modern eyes, at least—some awkward interludes. It was designed in three separate parts to simulate the administrative offices, garage compound and factory area of a middle-sized manufacturer (plate 8). These three elements are disparate in form and proportion, not only because they house quite different operations but also because Gropius, with inadequate funds, had to use the money and/or materials donated by Rhineland manufacturers in response to his plea. The steel bents of the factory area are employed with candor and directness: they yield the unobstructed span required and their unadorned profile gives the factory its distinction. The administrative block, while it has some justly famous features, is not so clearly organized or felicitously developed. The spiral concrete stairs at either end, cantilevered out from a central column and encased in a tubular glass curtain wall, are stunning tours de force. Inevitably they evoke a poetic image of industrial process: sun-flooded, immaculate, smoothly turning, they celebrate the quiet, impersonal efficiency of the machine. There is some awkwardness about the way in which the glass curtain wall returns around the ends of the block. But in modeling, transparency and floating detachment across the courtyard façade, this glass curtain goes far beyond the Fagus factory. In features such as these we see the power and originality of Gropius' work and can understand why they created such a sensation in that fateful summer of 1914.

The war put an end to this most promising phase of his career. An officer in the cavalry, he was called up at once. By the time his future wife, Alma Mahler, had heard about his Cologne success and written to congratulate him from Vienna, he had already been hospitalized from a bomb explosion. The war years might have been a trifle less tedious for him than for most European architects since he had a postwar project to dream about. For, as early as 1915, he had been called back from the front to an audience with the Grand Duke of Saxe-Weimar who (on van de Velde's recommendation) offered him the directorship of the Grand Ducal School of Arts and Crafts.

It is obvious that Gropius thought long and hard about this project, since he moved so swiftly and surely to create the *Weimar Staatliches Bauhaus* the moment he was free to do so. We have already seen why this creation of his was to be, in truth, a lever long enough to move the world. It was to occupy (in fact, devour) his time and energies for the next decade. Yet even during those years, he was a productive designer. The Germany of the immediate postwar was an inauspicious spot for any artist whose medium was as costly as an architect's. In the decade ending 1928, Gropius had only 47 architectural commissions; of these, only 23 materialized and several of them were exhibitions.[28] Among these, nevertheless, were to be some of his greatest works.

For Gropius, with his Protestant background and Prussian schooling, was never idle. Believing in "the common citizenship of all forms of creative work," he could design a door handle or a line of mass-produced furniture with as much concentration and zest as he would expend upon a great theater or a city plan. His imagination and versatility as an industrial designer had already been established before the war, when he had designed a self-propelled Diesel railway car, a sleeping car for the German Railway, steel furniture for a battleship and luxury furniture for a villa. His theoretical grasp of the problems of designing for industry is clear from articles which he wrote for the yearbooks of the *Werkbund,* of which he was an active member. In 1913 he was hailing the "monumental power" and "unacknowledged majesty" of the American grain silos: the anonymous works of practical men, they could nevertheless "stand comparison with the constructions of ancient Egypt." The following year he contributed an article on the design of "automobile and railroad car, steamship and sailing vessel, airship and airplane."[29] And after 1919, at the Bauhaus, there was literally no area of industrial design, from silver tablespoons to automobile bodies, in which Gropius was not active, both as head of the school and as a professional designer.

The range and mastery of his architecture during this period are demonstrated in three designs, only one of which was ever realized: the project for the Chicago Tribune Tower (1922); the building and staff housing for the Bauhaus at Dessau (1925–26); and the design for the Total Theater in Berlin (1927). Each of these is a classic prototype of its kind. The Tribune Tower design (plate 11), by its lucid rationality, exposes as sheer madness almost all the other eclectic entries in the competition, including the incredible Doric column of Loos (plate 12) and the Gothic prizewinner of Howells and Hood (plate 13). Even today this skyscraper of Gropius' stands head and shoulders above the current standard.

But it was the design of an entire new plant for the Bauhaus, when it moved from Weimar to Dessau, which challenged him to the greatest response of his entire career. This is perhaps to be expected since, of all his buildings, it was done for the client whose needs he knew most intimately. Like Jefferson at Charlottesville, he was the architect of the entire *institution,* its philosophy and curriculum no less than its physical envelope. And the Bauhaus complex is a beautiful demonstration of his conviction that "architects should conceive of buildings not as monuments but as receptacles for the flow of life which they have to serve."[30] The flow of Bauhaus life he knew most intimately; and if we marvel today at the effortless poise with which the five elements fit together—classrooms, administrative offices, workshops, social areas and dormitories—it is because the forms derived so surely from their functions. This is indeed a composition to which nothing can be added or subtracted. It is a classic precisely because Gropius has so completely abjured any personal indulgence—making himself, one might almost say, the pure vehicle or medium of the design process.

This same ability illuminates the third great project of this epoch—the Total Theater which he designed for Erwin Piscator. Here again, Gropius' knowledge of the problem was anything but superficial. Himself a devotee of all theatrical forms, he had many contacts in the field including men like Bertold Brecht and Kurt Weill who played and sang for him the savagely witty score of the *Three Penny Opera* before it opened in a Berlin theater. Theater and ballet played an important role in the Bauhaus: as early as 1923 Oscar Schlemmer taught a full range of theater subjects and was able to produce his avant-garde *Triadic Ballet,* with music, dancing sets and costumes by Bauhaus students. Gropius and Adolph Meyer had remodeled the municipal theater of Jena in that same year; and—though he was never to build any of them—Gropius had designed outstanding theaters for Halle (1927), Kharkov (1930) and the Palace of the Soviets in Moscow (1931). He was thus peculiarly well-equipped to respond to Piscator's unorthodox requirements. Basically, Piscator sought to destroy the artificial barrier which the proscenium interposes between actors and audience. He also sought convertibility, flexibility, anonymity, in the actual enclosure which would permit him the greatest freedom in staging productions. Gropius accepted these criteria wholeheartedly: in the Total Theater he designed an auditorium with many movable elements which permitted either an orthodox deep stage, a proscenium, a central arena-type stage or all three simultaneously (plates 54–61). In addition, he eliminated all conventional walls, replacing them with provisions for movable panels which could completely

Total Theater. Sketch by Gropius showing central stage
in position

envelope the audience, including transparent screens on which movies could be projected from the rear.

The Black Friday of 1927, which brought the fantastic German inflation to a halt, also killed the Total Theater. This must be reckoned as a permanent loss, for it would have brought to full professional maturity a theater which, even thirty years later, is still unrealized. But it was a great *succès d'estime* in Europe and, seven years later, afforded Gropius both the pretext and the means of escape from Hitler's Germany. He and his second wife, the former Ise Frank, were permitted to go to Rome to attend an international theater conference; from there they went into exile in London. At that conference, Gropius read a paper which not only showed his knowledge of the theater but also his special concept of the architect's responsibility:

> The task of the architect today, as I see it, is to create a great and flexible instrument which can respond in terms of light and space to every requirement of the theater producer: an instrument so impersonal that it never restrains [the producer] from giving his vision and imagination full play.[31]

Here he is demanding a quite extraordinary sublimation of the architect's own identity as a creative artist—a demand which all his great contemporaries would have found quite inacceptable. Indeed, it runs so counter to theater design from Palladio's *Teatro Olimpico* to Charles Garnier's Paris Opera (plate 56), that most architects would have found it incomprehensible. And yet, impossibly detached or insensitive as this demand might seem, it turns out that his "impersonal instrument" is aimed at maximum audience participation in the drama. His theater is to be an instrument as amenable and flexible as a great violin in the hands of an artist. "Its ingenious devices are merely means to attain the supreme goal—*to draw the spectator into the drama.*" It will abolish "the separation between the 'fictitious world' of the stage and the 'real world' of the audience . . . by erasing the distinction between 'this side' and 'that side' of the footlights."[32] Thus Gropius' theater is "a mobilization of all spatial means to rouse the spectator from his intellectual apathy, to assault and overwhelm him, to coerce him into participation in the play."[33] So it is the grave and self-effacing Gropius, and not the opulent Garnier, who emerges as the real protagonist of passionate involvement in the theater, the *Katharsis* of the Greeks.

From that theatrical conference in Italy Gropius and his wife went to England. However painful exile must have been for him personally, it did not seriously disturb the tenor of his work. He carried his great talent with him to England where, in association with Maxwell Fry, it flowered as gracefully in the Impington College buildings (plates 88, 89) as though it were a native. And it survived the much more radical transplantation to America in 1937. His own house outside Cambridge of that same year (plate 91) and the wartime housing project at New Kensington (plate 98) of 1941 show him responding felicitously to the new American environment. Other projects of the postwar period, however, seem to fall below the high standard which he himself had set. The Harvard Graduate Center (1949) seems oddly old-fashioned, close to being a cliché of his own earlier creations (plates 105–111). This stylistic disturbance might well have been due to the fact that, after 1945, Gropius was the senior partner of a large and growing office. His theories of collaborative design were being tested on a large scale and it is perhaps not surprising that the results have not always seemed completely consistent.

He must have been thinking of this period when, in 1959, he ruefully observed: "I have been a 'nobody's baby' during just those years of middle life which normally bring a man to the apex of his career, when seed sown earlier should have come to fruition."[34] It is true that conviction and fate had conspired to make him an artistic radical, a political exile and then an enemy alien from the age of 36 to that of 62. What is also true (and much less widely understood) is that a profound sense of social commitment had kept him a teacher when, in his heart, he wanted to be a designer![35] Only since his retirement in 1952 has he been able to devote his entire time and energy to design. And in this most recent phase we find him embarked upon one of the largest and most significant projects of his whole career—the new University at Bagdad (plates 124–135). Although this might have come to him "twenty years too late"[36] it nevertheless shows the seed of his lifetime coming to fruition. All those qualities we have come to associate with his architecture—its sobriety, its luminous rationality, its meticulous attention to functional necessity and immaculate solution of structural problems—all of these we find in the Bagdad designs. And we find something more: here, in the cradle of civilization, under the impact of an exotic culture and a desert climate, we find a kind of grave poetry emerging in his architecture, a statement at once more lyrical and more personal than he has usually permitted himself.

The quality which has distinguished his career from that of Wright or Mies has been its explicit social responsibility. This has had important consequences for his architecture, since he has always interpreted it to mean not merely the solution of socially urgent problems in architecture (e.g., housing and town planning) but also their expression in "a teachable, supra-individual language of form."[37] The pull of social reality, like the tropism which turns flowers toward the sun, has thus oriented Gropius away from the intimate, the personal, the subjective. This has necessarily restricted the color and passion with which, as an artist, he might otherwise have infused his works. But it is obvious that temperament also plays a part here: sheer rationality would have prevented his committing such acts of subjectivism as Taliesin or Ronchamp.

In such a philosophical attitude, of course, he occupies a position exactly opposite to that of Wright, Mies or Le Corbusier. For these men are, above everything else, *polemical* architects. Their buildings must be understood as they themselves understand them—that is, as the most powerful and persuasive statements they can formulate of a given artistic conviction. Not one of them could accept Gropius' "impersonal instrument" theory of architecture: the Guggenheim Museum, the Seagram Building, the chapel at Ronchamp—these are highly charged artistic acts, in which we may be sure that any conflict between container and contained is resolved in favor of the container. Not one of these men could have worked with collaborators, as Gropius does, because their very concept of creativity is so private. It is not that they are wrong or Gropius right: the world needs both kinds of architects desperately. But Gropius, drawing his analogies from the world of science and technology, has tried to cross a new frontier in architecture into areas where design by the individual genius is simply no longer possible.

For this reason, throughout his professional life, he has always had collaborators: Adolph Meyer in Germany from 1911 to 1924; Maxwell Fry in England (1934–37); Marcel Breuer in America (1937–41); and, since 1946, The Architects' Collaborative. That he made these associations always from a sense of duty rather than from any fear of his own powers is proved by the fact that the finest buildings he ever did—the purest, most consistent and flawless—were precisely those done in the only period when he was alone, after Meyer's tragic drowning in 1924. But we must remember that perfection of stylistic expression, while important for him, has never been decisive; and when it becomes simply a means of personal expression it is, for Gropius, an "arrogant misapprehension" of the architect's task. That task is discharged only when he brings "inert materials to life by relating them to the human being. Thus conceived, his creation is an act of love."[38]

This conviction that collaboration in design was both inevitable and good has led him to devote much time and energy to the discovery and development of new talent, not only as students but also as colleagues. Thus, while some of the Bauhaus staff had established reputations when Gropius engaged them, these reputations would have been narrowly circumscribed by the avant-garde of Berlin's intelligentsia. Johannes Itten, the Viennese painter whose basic design course Gropius considered a cornerstone of the school, was an unknown when Alma Mahler introduced him: Klee, Feininger and Kandinsky came to be widely recognized only in later years. He engaged the young Moholy-Nagy immediately after he saw his exhibition (that of the "telephoned" paintings) in 1922. He haunted the cafés and galleries of Berlin in his search for talent: indeed, one of his first acts after the armistice was to organize, at the Berlin gallery of J. B. Neumann, a show of the works of young, unknown architects. It was here that the work of Eric Mendelsohn, among others, was first exposed. Breuer, first a student at the Bauhaus, later became one of Gropius' most trusted collaborators. And many of the world's most prominent younger architects today were his students at Harvard. Chester Nagel expressed their common sentiment when he wrote:

> We who have been Gropius' students can say gratefully that he has shown us a place in society; that he has taught us that mechanization and individual freedom are not incompatible; that he has explained to us the possibilities and values of communal action.[39]

And still another strand has bound Gropius to the factual and objective: his perennial concern with the impact of industrialism upon architecture. This was changing the architect's work at every level, whether in the new design problems it posed, the new materials in which they might be executed, or the new methods by which it might be done. One obvious evidence of this lifelong concern has been his work in mass housing (a new design problem) and in prefabrication (a new method of accomplishing it). His pioneering work in German housing is sufficiently well known: the workers' housing at Toerten, Dessau of 1926–27, (plate 72); the proposed high-rise flats at Wannsee of 1931 (plate 84); the middle-class apartments at Siemensstadt, 1929 (plate 78). But long before this he had become interested in prefabrication. As early as 1909 he drafted a proposal for the application of advanced industrial techniques to the production of standardized panels out of which a variety of houses could be assembled. He returned to this theme in Weimar in 1921 and again in the Toerten houses in 1927. He designed and built for the 1927 Werkbund Housing Exhibition a lightweight prefab with metal skeleton and asbestos and cork walls. He designed another prefab for a German manufacturer in 1931 (plates 74–76); and still another for the General Panel Corporation in America in 1945.[40]

All during the German years, Gropius made time-and-motion studies of labor-saving devices in both the construction and the use of his houses. This was another transfer from industry of the sorts of techniques which, decades later, were to become a commonplace in architecture. Thus, whether it is the site photographs recording the erection techniques at Toerten (with mechanization so primitive that it seems a little sad today) or the movies of the labor-saving features of the cabinet work in the Dessau faculty houses, we are face to face with real pioneering. Its very familiarity is, again, a proof of Gropius' prescience. And it was this interest in *process* which protected both Gropius and the Bauhaus from the kind of sterile formalism which has overwhelmed so much industrial design.

3. *GROPIUS, THE SOCIAL CRITIC*

THE VERY STRUCTURE of his mind has always propelled Gropius into social speculation. Unlike Wright or Mies, he was never able to focus his whole attention upon the design of the individual building to the exclusion of its social setting. Like Le Corbusier, he was always compelled to examine the larger organism of which the individual building was but a cell. As he put it:

> My idea of the architect as the coordinator—whose business is to unify the various formal, technical, social and economic problems that arise in connection with building—inevitably led me on, step by step, from study of the function of the house to that of the street; from the street to the town; and finally to the still vaster implications of regional and national planning.[41]

Not only was he led on, step by step, to examine the fabric of modern society: he was forced to comment on it. And though this often led him into exposed positions, it is to his credit that he always chose the principled (rather than the merely expedient) course of action. Rather than submit to the reactionary demands of the Weimar government in 1925, he moved the Bauhaus—lock, stock and barrel—to Dessau. When fundamental differences between himself and the city government appared in 1928, it was he who resigned rather than wreck the Bauhaus. And in 1934, rather than face life in a Hitler dominated Germany, he left his homeland forever.

The same kind of forthrightness has marked his public positions as an American citizen. Thus when *The Saturday Evening Post,* that bastion of middle-class American complacency, gave him the chance to speak his mind, it was the "curse" of American conformism that he chose to attack:

> Our biggest man-made objects—our cities—have steadily grown more chaotic and ugly, despite brilliant individual contributions. . . . For all the heroic efforts of conservationists, a good deal of our loveliest countryside is being bulldozed out of existence, a sacrifice to commercial exploitation . . . regional character and community spirit [wage] a losing battle against the conformity imposed by mass production . . . and the natural feeling for quality and appropriateness is dissipated in the giddy tumble from novelty to novelty.[42]

Nor has he hesitated to speak out on other shortcomings of American democracy. When he went to New Orleans to accept the American Institute of Architects Gold Medal, he found himself in a city which dictated a racially segregated convention. Though this had caused acute discomfort among some of the architects, Gropius was one of the few to protest publicly. He liked the city which in many ways reminded him of the cities of his European youth; and he hoped he "could live long enough to attend a future AIA convention from which the shadow of segregation, which now so deeply disturbs our minds, has been at last removed."[43]

The ferocity of the attacks which had been leveled against him in the Bauhaus, even in the pre-Hitler days in Weimar, seems hard to explain in rational terms. For Gropius was never other than what he appeared to be—a consistent and principled democrat. Certainly, the socio-political perspectives implicit in his early manifestoes seem modest enough. The individual might be "enslaved" and his society "disordered": yet he felt that any solution depended upon "a change in the individual's attitude toward his work, not on the betterment of his outward circumstances . . . Only work which is the product of inner compulsion can have spiritual meaning."[44] At a distance of four decades, this sounds like an almost Tolstoyan doctrine of personal regeneration: it is not even a call to simple trade unionism, much less to radical political action. Some of his defenders tried to point this out, in the days when the Bauhaus was under the most savage attacks. One of them said that the Bauhaus manifesto "clearly stated that harmonious creation is an ethical problem to be solved by the individual . . ."[45] A blunter rejection of Marxism and kindred Utopias is inconceivable.

Non-Marxist it might have been; but Utopian it certainly was—and this alone was enough to bring down upon it the blind and bloody wrath of the Hitlerites. Yet the plans of those early days are suffused with a youthful idealism which seems, in retrospect, like Eden before the Fall. Thus we read, in one prospectus, that "a vegetable and fruit farm, leased from the state, was worked by the Bauhaus and [this] made the kitchen independent of price fluctuations in the markets. A plan was being evolved for single houses and apartments . . . the construction of these community buildings was to be directed by the Bauhaus and was to provide contracts for its workshops."[46] It all sounds more like the Brook Farm of Transcendentalist New England than the Germany of the Dawes Plan.

In an effort to protect (or at least to isolate) the school from the political convulsions around it, Gropius forbade any political activity on the part of staff or student body.[47] Finally, since so much of the Rightist wrath seemed focused on him personally, Gropius tried to deflect it from the Bauhaus by resigning as director. But none of this saved them from the Nazis. For though the political program of the Bauhaus might extend no further left than a kind of mild co-operativism, its esthetic program was uncompromisingly radical. This the fascist madmen understood. The Bauhaus stood for the complete liberation of the creative personality from the servile eclecticism of the past. It called for the fullest and freest examination of the fundamentals of design and for the reconstruction of the world of visual form. In this capacity, it had consistently and courageously attracted some of the most advanced artists in Europe. From a practical point of view it was, as Giedion has pointed out

> . . . sheer madness to jeopardize one's reputation and position by the appointment of artists such as Klee, Kandinsky, Feininger, Schlemmer and Moholy-Nagy as government servants in a state institution: artists whose significance was appreciated only by a very small circle and whose work and outlook excited the strongest expressions of outrage, abuse and detestation throughout Germany . . .[48]

Moreover, in its publications it espoused movements like Cubism and Non-Objectivism, foreign artists like Mondrian, van Doesburg and Malevich. This uncompromising policy drew to its defense all that was healthiest in German culture: the architects Behrens, Mies van der Rohe, Poelzig; the novelists Werfel, Sudermann, Hauptmann; the painter Kokoschka; the composer Schönberg; the producer Reinhardt; the scientist Einstein. In short, Gropius stood—then, as always—on the side of life: this the Nazis understood and could not forgive.

In 1954, at the age of 71, Walter Gropius visited Japan for the first time. There he found a modern architecture which his life's work had done much to create. But there, also, he was face to face with that great body of traditional art and architecture which had done so much to reshape the artistic theories of the Europe of his youth: again the elliptical confrontation of made and maker. In that old architecture he saw expressed the principle he had always advocated: endless variety within a fundamental unity, a rich diversity which was not hostile to the organic whole. "For the first time in my life," he tells us with unwitting poignancy, "I felt myself with the majority."[49] It is sad to think that he should ever have felt so isolated, for he has always tried to act in the interests of the many, the multitude. Few creative personalities in our period have sought as consistently as he to speak for the majority. Though there may have been many times when it seemed he fought alone, he should be assured he is alone no longer. More perhaps than he can ever know, a majority—a majority of his making—is with him now.

The Notes to the Text begin on page 113.

1a. Peter Behrens, Turbine Factory, Berlin, 1910.

1b. Frank Lloyd Wright, Larkin Building, Buffalo, New York, 1904.

1c. Louis Sullivan, Schlesinger-Meyer Store, Chicago, 1899-1904.

1. Fagus Shoe Last Factory, Alfeld an der Leine, 1911 (with Adolf Meyer).

2. Fagus Factory. Exterior

3. Fagus Factory Entrance.

4. Diesel Locomotive, 1913

5. Sleeping Car for German Railways, 1914.

6. Werkbund Exhibition Machine Hall, Cologne, 1914. Entrance to workshops.

7. Werkbund Exhibition, Cologne. Office building, view from court.

8. Werkbund Exhibition, Cologne. Office building and machine hall.

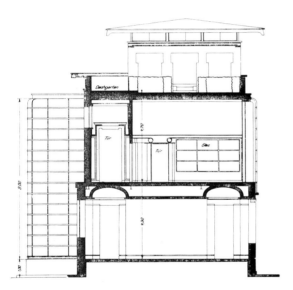

9. Werkbund Exhibition, Cologne. Section, glass-walled staircase of office building.

10. Werkbund Exhibition, Cologne. Office building staircase.

11. Chicago Tribune Tower Competition Entry, 1922 (with Adolf Meyer).

12. Adolf Loos, Tribune Tower Competition Entry, 1922.

13. Howells and Hood, Winning Entry, Tribune Tower Competition, 1922. (Built)

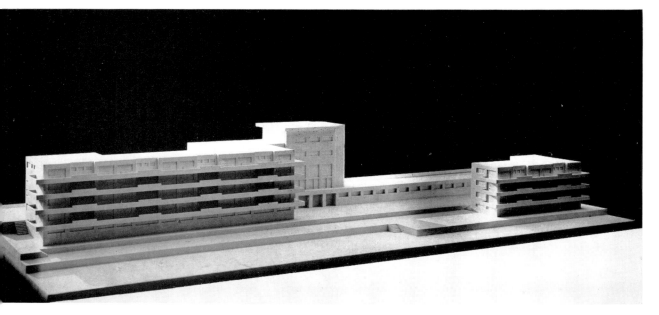

14. Academy of Philosophy, Erlangen, 1924 (Project, with Adolf Meyer). Model.

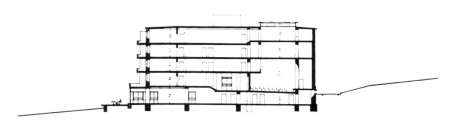

15. Academy of Philosophy. Section.

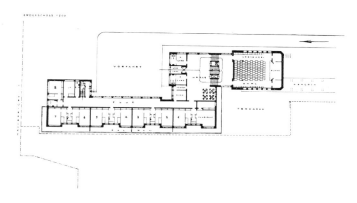

16. Academy of Philosophy. Plan.

17. Bauhaus Buildings, Dessau, 1926. Photograph by Lyonel Feininger.

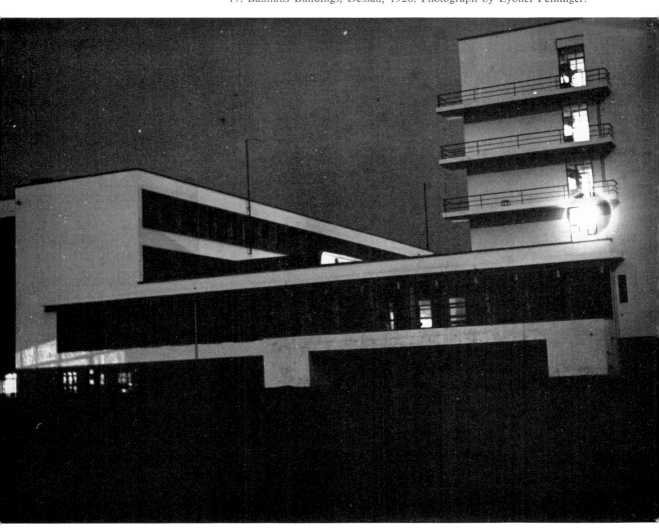

18. Bauhaus, Dessau. Workshop wing at left, student's studios at right.

19. Bauhaus, Dessau. Student's studios in foreground.

20. Bauhaus, Dessau. Plan.

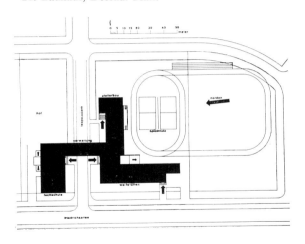

21. Bauhaus, Dessau. Administration wing over the street, connecting the school divisions.

22. Bauhaus, Dessau. Interior, director's office.

23. Bauhaus, Dessau. Interior, corridor and stairs.

24. Bauhaus, Dessau. Interior, auditorium.

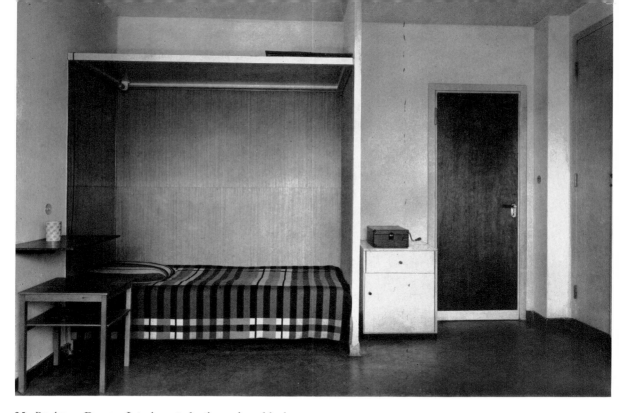

25. Bauhaus, Dessau. Interior, student's work-and-bedroom.

26. Bauhaus, Dessau. Interior, workshop.

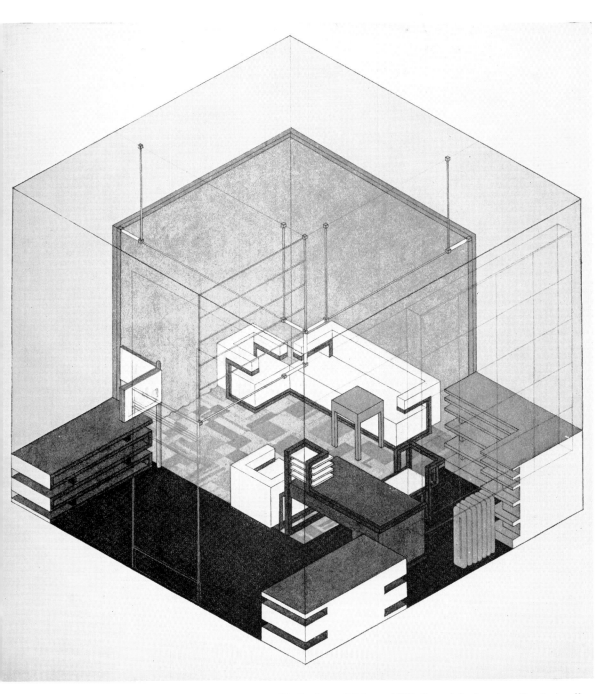

27. Bauhaus, Weimar, 1923. Isometric drawing, director's office.

28. Margarete Willers, Hand-woven fabric

29. Marianne Brandt, Metal utensils.

30. Marcel Breuer, Tubular steel chair.

31. Ceiling lamp.

32. Theodore Bogler, Porcelain ware.

33. Marianne Brandt, Metal utensils.

34. Oskar Schlemmer, Ballet Figures.

35. Gropius House, Bauhaus, Dessau, 1925.

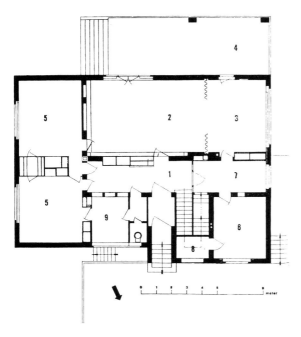

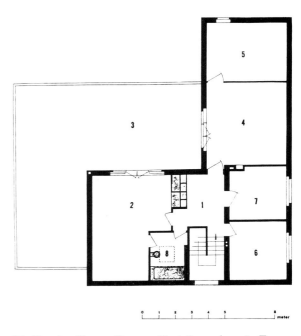

36. Gropius House, Dessau. Ground floor plan: 1. Foyer, 2. Living room, 3. Dining room, 4. Terrace, 5. Bedroom, 6. Kitchen, 7. Service pantry, 8. Food pantry, 9. Bath.

37. Gropius House, Dessau. First floor plan: 1. Foyer, 2. Guest living-bedroom, 3. Roof terrace, 4. Studio, 5. Storage, 6. Maid, 7. Laundry, 8. Bath.

8. Gropius House, Dessau. Veranda outside dining room.

39. Gropius House, Dessau. Dining room.

40. Faculty Housing, Bauhaus, Dessau, 1925. "Double House."

42. Moholy-Nagy House, Bauhaus, Dessau, 1925. Studio.

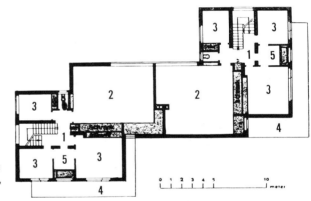

43a. Faculty Housing, Dessau. Ground floor plan:
1. Foyer, 2. Living room, 3. Dining room, 4. Terrace,
5. Kitchen, 6. Storage.

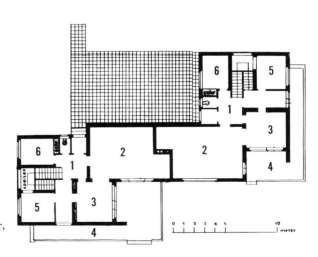

43b. Faculty Housing, Dessau. First floor plan: 1. Foyer,
2. Studio, 3. Bedroom, 4. Balcony, 5. Bath.

44. Municipal Employment Office, Dessau, 1927-28.

45. Employment Office, Dessau. Section.

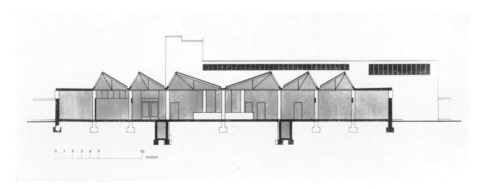

46. Employment Office, Dessau. Interior.

47. Employment Office, Dessau. Isometric drawing.

48. Standard furniture for Feder Stores, Berlin, 1927.

49. Standard furniture for Feder Stores.

50. Werkbund Exhibition, Paris, 1930.

51. Building Exhibition, Berlin, 1931. Gymnasium, swimming pool at right.

52. Alder Cabriolet, 1930.

53. Alder Cabriolet. Interior, showing reclining seats.

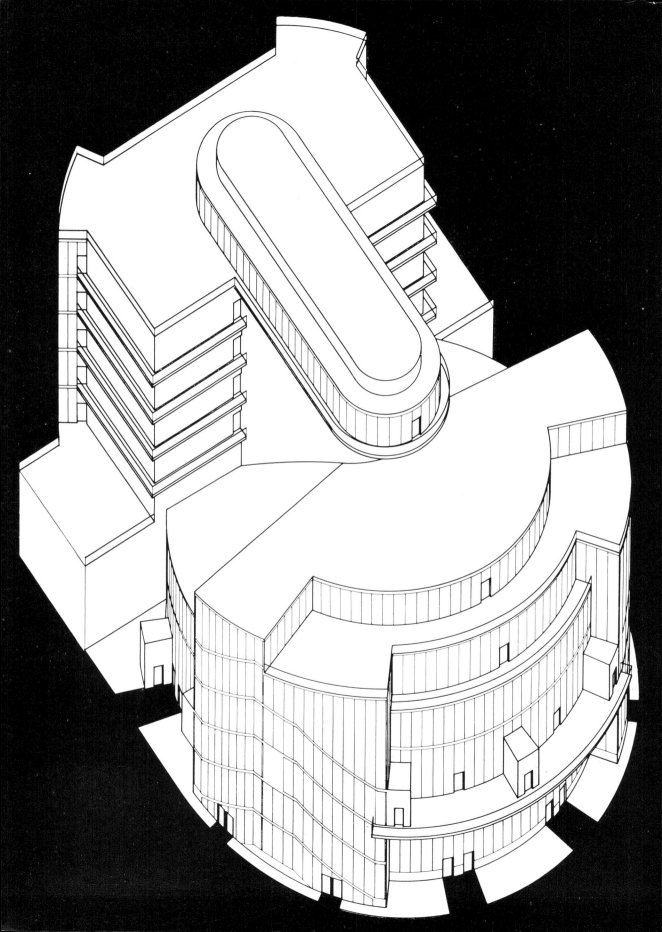

55. Total Theater, Model, side elevation.

56. Charles Garnier, Opera House, Paris, 1861-74. Interior looking toward proscenium.

57. Total Theater. Sketch, proscenium stage in position.

Total Theater, 1927 (Project). Isometric drawing (opposite page).

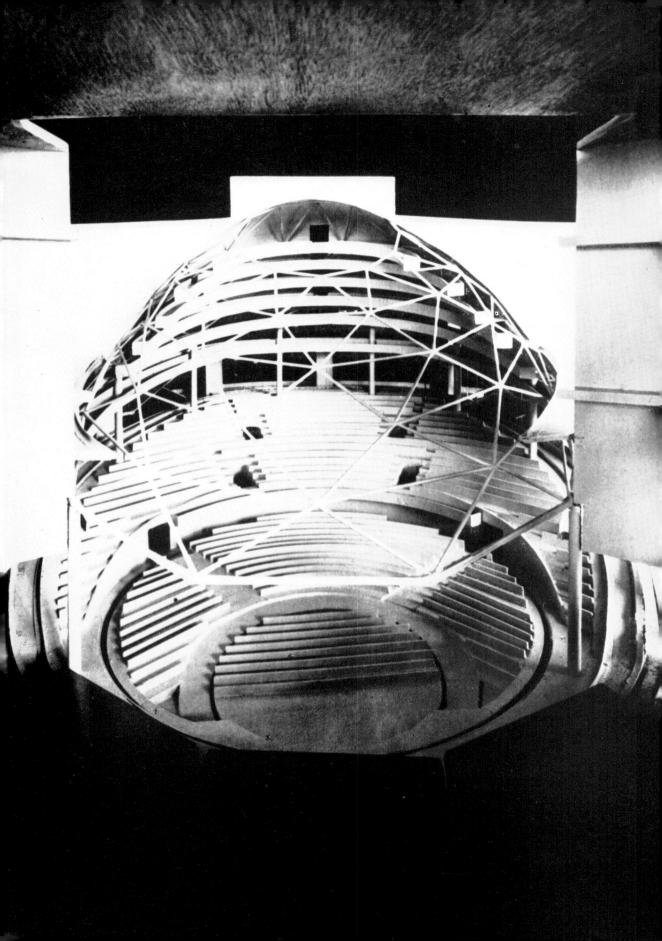

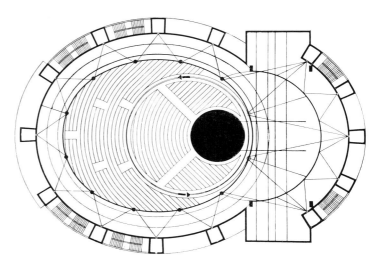

59. Total Theater. Plan, proscenium stage in position.

tal Theater. Model, section (opposite page).

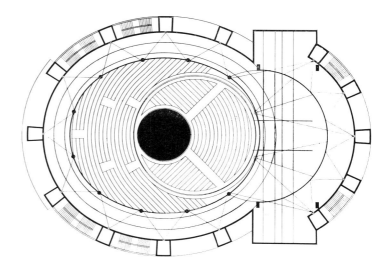

60. Total Theater. Plan, arena stage in position.

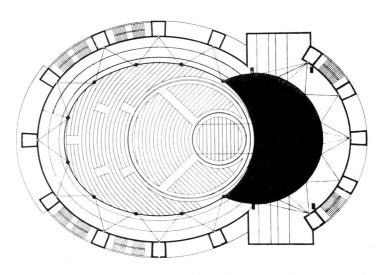

61. Total Theater. Plan, deep stage in position.

62. Ukranian State Theater, Kharkov, 1930 (Project). Perspective

массовый центр

63. Ukranian State Theater. Plan.

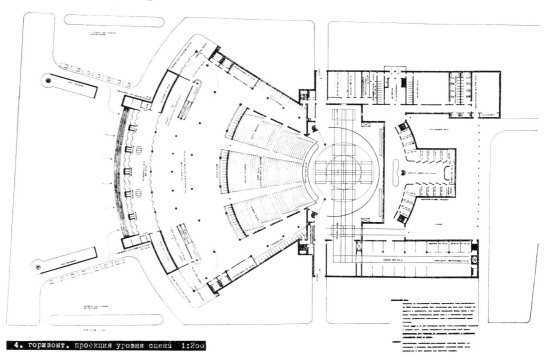

64. Palace of the Soviets, Moscow, 1931 (Project). Model.

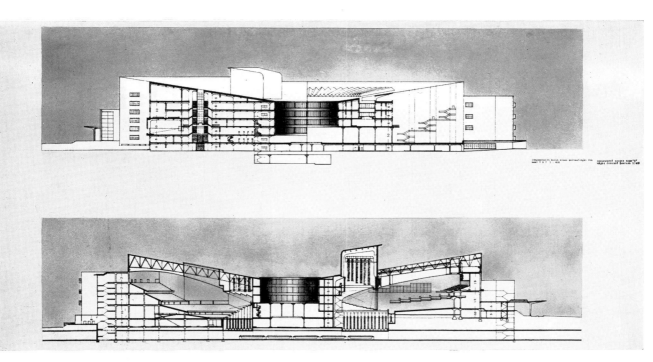

65. Palace of the Soviets. Longitudinal sections.

66. Palace of the Soviets. Plan.

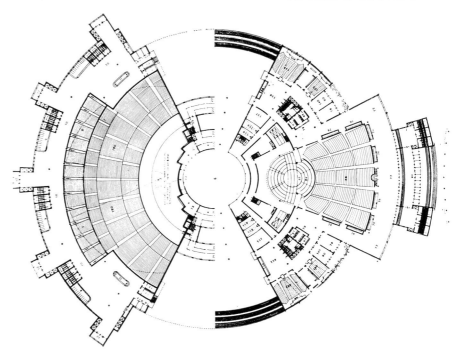

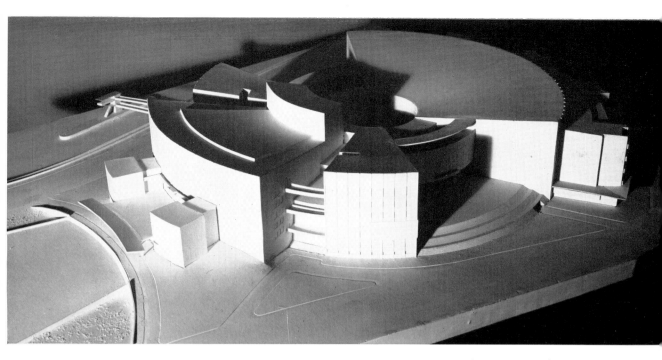

67. Palace of the Soviets. Model.

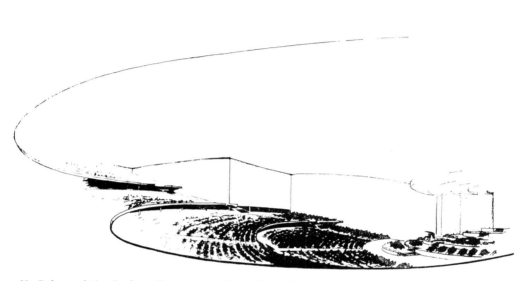

68. Palace of the Soviets. Sketch, assembly hall interior.

69. Palace of the Soviets. Sketch, theater entrance.

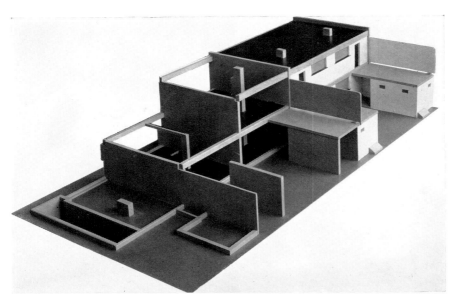

70. Toerten Housing, Dessau, 1926-27. Model, construction sequence.

71. Toerten Housing. Isometric drawing, row houses.

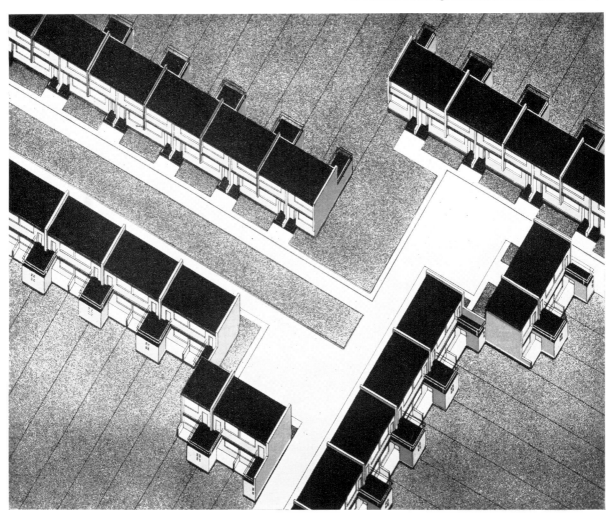

72. Toerten Housing. Row houses.

73. Weissenhof Housing, Werkbund Exhibition, Stuttgart, 1927. Prefabricated house.

74. Prefabricated Copper House. Construction, assembly of walls.

75. Prefabricated Copper House. View of terrace.

76. Prefabricated Copper House. Exterior.

77. Prefabricated Copper Houses. Plans: left, basic house; center, two rooms added; right, four rooms added.

A

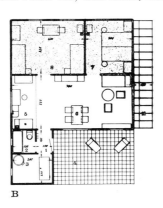

B

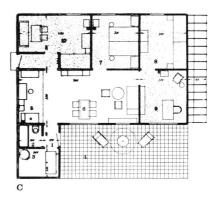

C

78. Siemensstadt Housing, Berlin, 1929.

wohnfl. 69 qm

siedlung siemensstadt berlin,

79. Siemensstadt Housing. Elevations, plan.

80. Siemensstadt Housing.

81. Siemensstadt Housing. Outside corridor.

82. Eleven Story Slab Apartment Blocks, 1931 (Project).

83. Eleven Story Slab. Model.

84. Wannsee Apartment Blocks, Berlin, 1931 (Project).

85. Wannsee Apartments. Site plan.

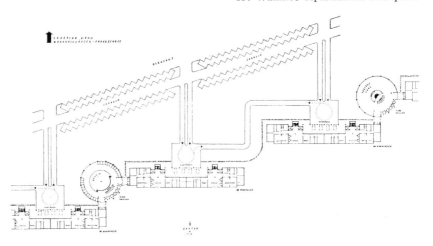

86. Wannsee Apartments. Typical floor plan.

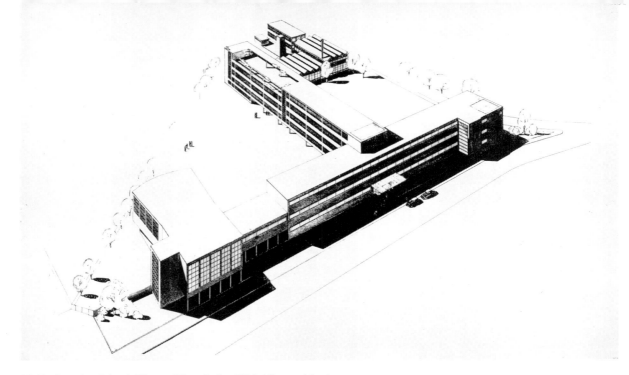

87. Engineering School, Hagen, Westphalia, 1929 (Competition).

88. Impingten College, Cambridgeshire, 1936 (with Maxwell Fry). Exterior, assembly hall

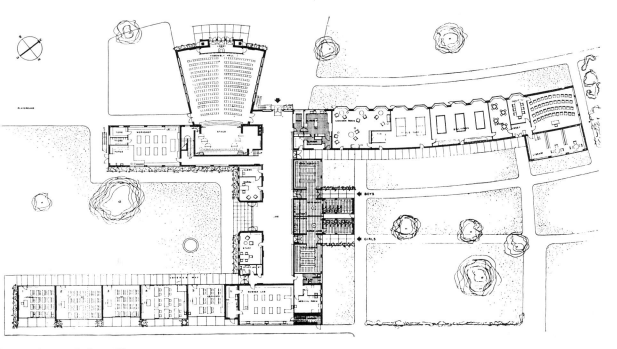

89. Impington College. Plan

90. Impington College. Exterior, classroom wing.

91. Gropius House, Lincoln, Massachusetts, 1937 (with Marcel Breuer).

92. Gropius House, Lincoln. Ground floor and first floor plans.

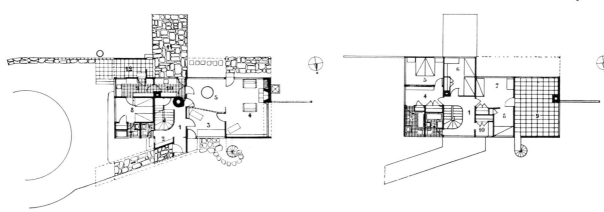

93. Gropius House, Lincoln. Exterior from south.

94. Gropius House, Lincoln. Living-dining room.

95. Chamberlain House, Sudbury, Massachusetts, 1939 (with Marcel Breuer).

96. Howlett House, Belmont, Massachusetts, 1949 (with The Architects' Collaborative).

97. Howlett House. Interior.

98. New Kensington Housing, near Pittsburgh, Pennsylvania, 1941 (with Marcel Breuer).

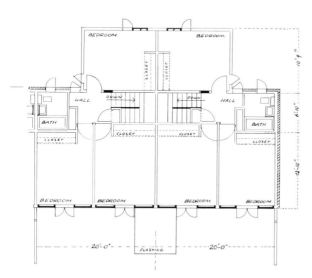

99. New Kensington Housing. Plan, upper floor of row house.

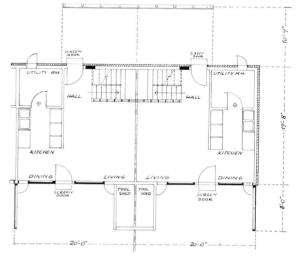

100. New Kensington Housing. Plan, ground floor of row house.

101. New Kensington Housing. Row houses.

102. New Kensington Housing. Site plan.

103. Black Mountain College, Lake Eden, North Carolina, 1939 (Project, with Marcel Breuer).

104. Black Mountain College. Plan.

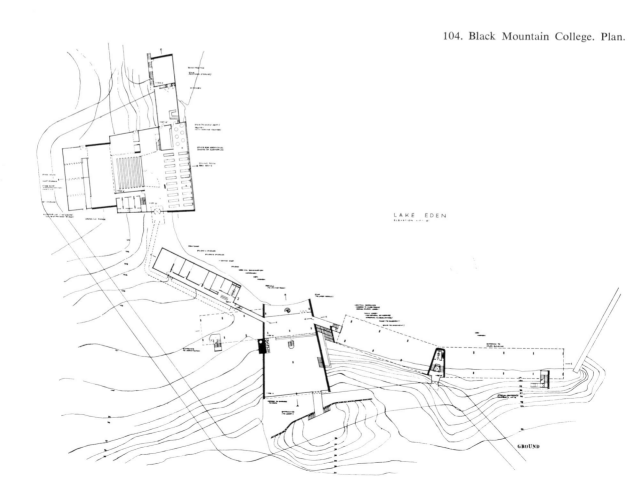

105. Harvard Graduate Center, Cambridge, Massachusetts, 1949 (with The Architects' Collaborative).

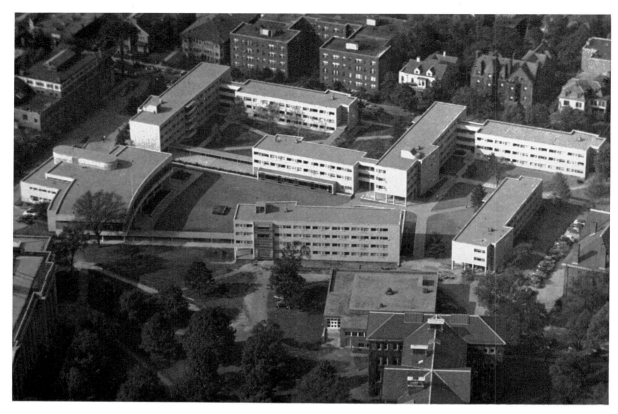

106. Harvard Graduate Center. Air view.

107. Harvard Graduate Center. Plan.

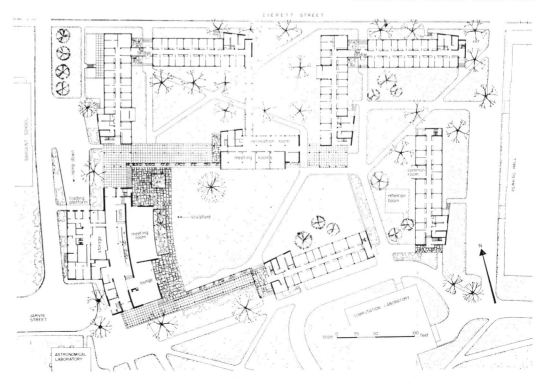

108. Harvard Graduate Center. Dormitories.

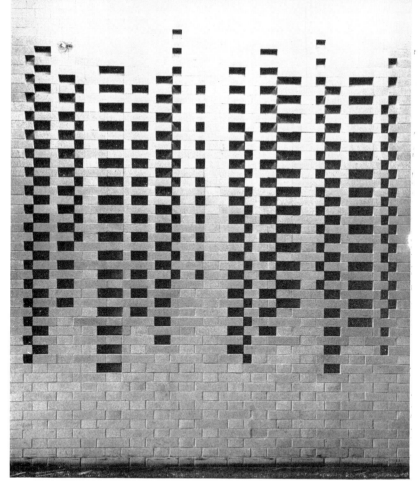

109. Harvard Graduate Center. Brick mural by Josef Albers, Harkness Commons.

110. Harvard Graduate Center. Glazed tile design by Herbert Bayer, Harkness Commons entrance hall.

111. Harvard Graduate Center. Mural by Joan Miro, main dining room.

112. McCormick Office Building, Chicago, 1953 (Project, with the Architects' Collaborative, Arthur Myhrum, Associate). Model.

113. American Association for the Advancement of Science Building, Washington, D. C., 1952 (Project, with The Architects' Collaborative). Model.

114. Boston Back Bay Center, 1953, (associated with Boston Center Architects). Model.

115. Boston Center. Aerial view, showing projected location.

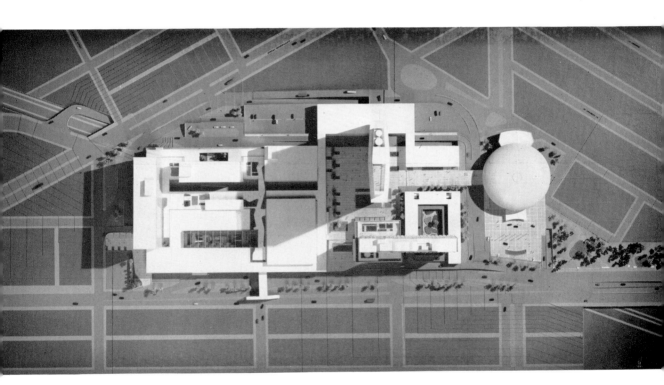

117. Boston Center. Model, seen from above.

116. Boston Center. Model, from the northwest (opposite page).

118. United States Embassy, Athens (with The Architects' Collaborative). (Under construction) Rendering, exterior detail.

119. U. S. Embassy, Athens. Model, seen from above.

120. U. S. Embassy, Athens. Construction.

121. U. S. Embassy, Athens. Construction, interior courtyard.

122. Rudow-Buckow Housing Development, West Berlin (Project, with The Architect's Collaborative; Partners in charge: Walter Gropius, Benjamin Thompson). Model, seen from above.

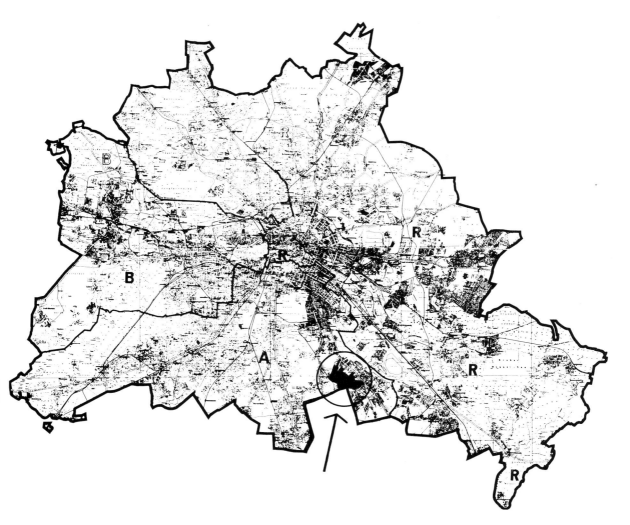

123. Rudow-Buckow. Map of Berlin showing projected location.

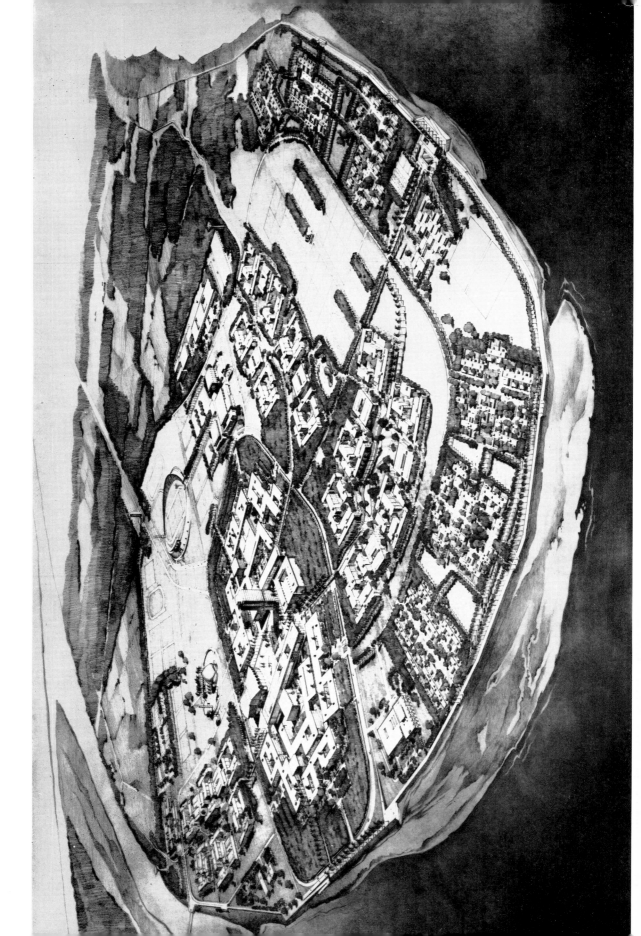

125. Bagdad University. Model, buildings in central area seen from southeast.

126. Bagdad University. Model, central area with administration building in foreground.

127. Bagdad University. Auditorium, south elevation.

128. Bagdad University. Library, academic area.

129. Bagdad University. Model, view toward administration building from southwest.

130. Bagdad University. Central area, view toward south from administration entry court.

131. Bagdad University. Mosque.

132. Bagdad University. Academic area, typical court.

133. Bagdad University. Entrance gate.   134. Bagdad University. Dormatories, narrow walking street.

135. Bagdad University. Academic Court.

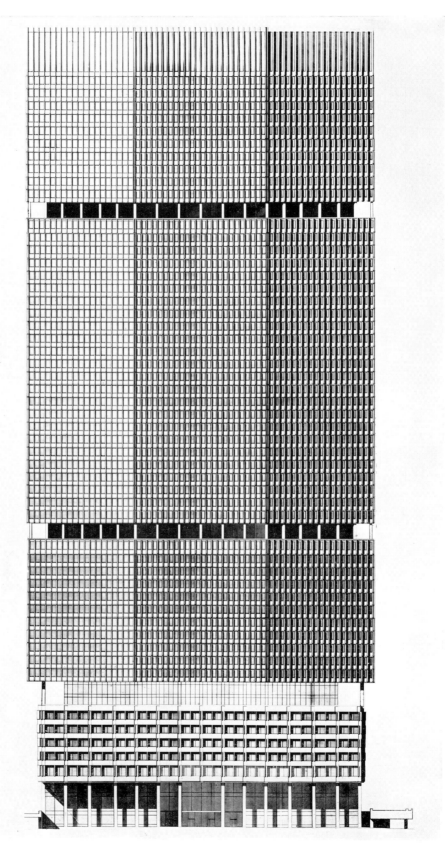

136. Grand Central City Building, New York (under construction). Walter Gropius (The Architects' Collaborative), Pietro Belluschi, Consultants; with Emery Roth and Sons. Front elevation.

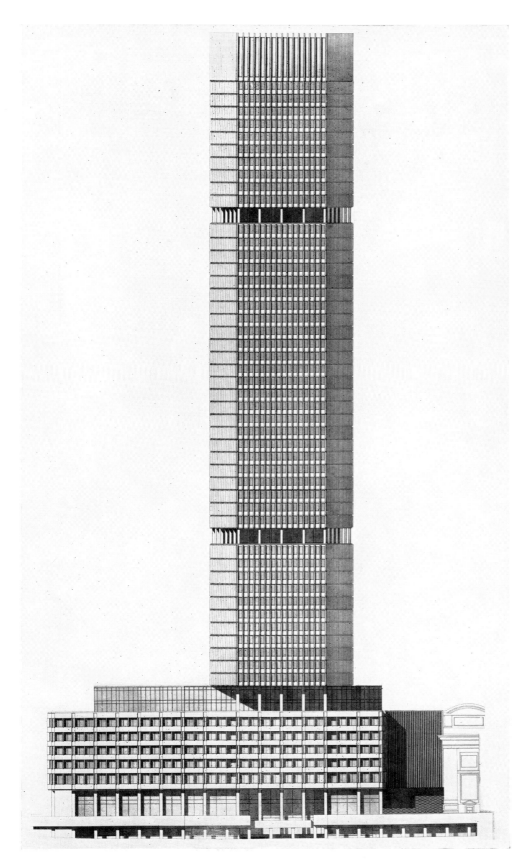

137. Grand Central City Building. Side elevation.

138. Grand Central City Building. Seen looking north on Park Avenue.

NOTES

1. Personal interview, Cambridge, April, 1960.
2. The contract was signed April 1, 1919. Alma Mahler Werfel, *And the Bridge is Love,* Harcourt, Brace, New York, 1957, p. 134.
3. The contract, signed under the regime of King Faisal, was renewed by the Republic of Iraq after the king's assassination.
4. Personal interview, Cambridge, February, 1960.
5. *Programm des Staatlichen Bauhauses,* Weimar, 1919.
6. Walter Gropius, *Scope of Total Architecture,* Harper, New York, 1955, pp. 18-19.
7. *Programm,* op. cit.
8. Herbert Bayer, Ise and Walter Gropius, *Bauhaus: 1919-1928,* The Museum of Modern Art, New York, 1938, p. 27.
9. *Ibid.,* p. 29.
10. *Ibid.,* p. 127.
11. *Ibid.,* p. 30.
12. *Ibid.,* p. 28.
13. *Ibid.,* p. 24.
14. Bauhaus curriculum and teaching methods were successfully transplanted by Moholy-Nagy in the same year when he established the *New Bauhaus* in Chicago. Reorganized in 1939 as the *School of Design* and again in 1944 as the *Institute of Design,* it is now a department of the Illinois Institute of Technology.
15. *Scope of Total Architecture,* op. cit., p. 3.
16. *Ibid.,* pp. xvii ff.
17. *Bauhaus,* op. cit., p. 11
18. Translation by Roger Banham, *Architectural Review,* London, February, 1957, Vol. 121, pp. 85-88.
19. From the catalog for the exhibition, *Unbekannte Architekten veranstaltet vom Arbeitsrat für Kunst,* Berlin, April, 1919.
20. Sibyl Moholy-Nagy, *Moholy-Nagy: A Biography,* New York, Harper, 1950, p. 31.
21. *Ibid.,* p. 19.
22. *Bauhaus,* op. cit., p. 22.
23. *Scope,* op. cit., p. 15.
24. *Ibid.,* p. 91.
25. Letter to the author, July 22, 1960.
26. *Scope,* op. cit., p. 92.
27. *Ibid.,* p. 6.
28. According to S. Giedion, *Walter Gropius: Work and Teamwork,* Reinhold, New York, 1954, p. 233.

29. *Ibid.,* p. 22.
30. *Scope,* op. cit., p. 93.
31. Giedion, op. cit., p. 63.
32. *Ibid.,* pp. 64, 65.
33. Moholy-Nagy, op. cit., p. 53.
34. Gropius, *AIA Journal,* Washington, August, 1959, p. 80.
35. Personal interview, Cambridge, May, 1960.
36. *Ibid.*
37. Gropius, "The Curse of Conformity," *Saturday Evening Post,* Philadelphia, June 6, 1958, pp. 18, 19ff.
38. Gropius, *Architecture and Design in the Age of Science,* Spiral Press, New York, 1952.
39. Chester Nagel, "Walter Gropius et son Ecole," *L'Architecture d'Aujourd'hui,* Paris, no. 28, February, 1950.
40. Gropius' work in prefabrication has been excellently summarized by Gilbert Herbert (*South African Architectural Record,* December, 1955, pp. 30-37).
41. Gropius, *The New Architecture and the Bauhaus,* Faber and Faber, London, 1935, p. 67.
42. "The Curse of Conformity," op. cit.
43. Gropius, *AIA Journal,* op. cit., p. 81.
44. *Bauhaus,* op. cit., p. 22.
45. *Ibid.,* p. 96.
46. *Ibid.,* p. 74.
47. *Ibid.,* p. 92.
48. Giedion, op. cit., p. 27.
49. Personal interview, Cambridge, February, 1960.

SELECTED CHRONOLOGICAL LIST OF BUILDINGS AND PROJECTS

1910–11   Fagus Works, Alfeld a.d. Leine (with Adolf Meyer)

1914   Werkbund Exhibition, Cologne

1922   Chicago Tribune Office Building, Chicago (with Adolf Meyer) (Competition)

1924   Academy of Philosophy, Erlangen (with Adolf Meyer) (Project)

1925–26   Bauhaus Buildings, Dessau

1925   Bauhaus Faculty Quarters, Dessau

1926   Toerten Housing, Dessau

1926–27   Weissenhof Prefabricated House, Werkbund Exhibition, Stuttgart

1927   Total Theater (Project)

1927–28   Municipal Employment Office, Dessau

1929   Engineering School, Hagen, Westphalia (Project)

1929–30   Housing Development, Berlin-Siemensstadt

1930   Werkbund Exhibition, Paris
           German Building Exhibition, Berlin
           Eleven Story Slab Building (Project)
           Ukrainian State Theater, Kharkov (Project)

1931   Wannsee Slab Buildings (Project)
           Prefabricated Copper House, Finow, Germany
           Soviet Palace, Moscow (Project)

1934   Non-Ferrous Metals Exhibition, Berlin (with Joost Schmidt)

1936   Impington College, Cambridgeshire (with Maxwell Fry)

1937   Gropius House, Lincoln, Massachusetts (with Marcel Breuer)

1939   Chamberlain House, Sudbury, Massachusetts (with Marcel Breuer)

1941   New Kensington Housing, near Pittsburgh, Pennsylvania (with Marcel Breuer)

1949   Howlett House, Belmont, Massachusetts
Harvard University Graduate Center, Cambridge, Massachusetts (with The Architects' Collaborative)

1952   Office Building for the American Association for the Advancement of Science, Washington, D.C. (with The Architects' Collaborative) (Project)

1953   Office Building for McCormick & Co., Chicago (with The Architects' Collaborative) (Project)
Boston Back Bay Center, Boston (associated with Boston Center Architects) (Project)

Work in Progress with The Architects' Collaborative:
United States Embassy, Athens (under construction)
University of Bagdad, Iraq
Housing Development, Buckow-Rudow, Berlin

Grand Central City Building, New York (*with Emery Roth Associates and Pietro Belluschi*) (under construction)

CHRONOLOGY

1883 Born May 18, Berlin

1903–07 Studied architecture in the Universities of Charlottenburg-Berlin and Munich

1907–10 Chief Assistant to Professor Peter Behrens, Berlin

1910 Own architectural practice, Berlin

1918 Director of the Grand Ducal Saxon School of Applied Arts and the Grand Ducal Academy of Arts; united these two schools under the name "Staatliches Bauhaus, Weimar"

1925 Continued as Director of the same Institute, which he moved to Dessau, Anhalt, under the name "Bauhaus Dessau." Title of Professor conferred by the Government of Anhalt

1928 Resumed private practice in Berlin
    Visited the United States

1929 Doctor of Engineering Degree (Honorary) awarded by the Hannover Institute of Technology

1929–57 Vice President of the International Congresses of Modern Architecture (CIAM), Zurich

1934–37 Private practice in London in partnership with architect Maxwell Fry

1937 Professor of Architecture in the Graduate School of Design, Harvard University, Cambridge

1938–52 Chairman of the Department of Architecture, Graduate School of Design, Harvard University
    Member of the American Institute of Architects

1938–43   Architectural practice in partnership with Marcel Breuer

1942   Master of Arts Degree (Honorary) conferred by Harvard University
           Honorary member of Phi Beta Kappa (Harvard Chapter)

1942–52   Vice President of the General Panel Corporation, New York

1943   *Socio Honorario, La Sociedad de Arquitectos Mexicanos*

1944   Fellow of the American Academy of Arts and Sciences
           Member of the American Society of Planners and Architects

1946   Formed "The Architects' Collaborative," Cambridge

1951   Doctor of Science Degree (Honorary) conferred by Western Reserve
           University, Cleveland, Ohio
           Gold Medal of Honor, the Architectural League of New York

1952   Professor Emeritus, Harvard University

1953   Doctor of Arts Degree (Honorary) conferred by Harvard University
           Doctor of Architecture Degree (Honorary) conferred by North Carolina
           State College
           Grand Prix International d'Architecture, "Premio Matarazzo," Mata-
           razzo Foundation, São Paulo, Brazil
           Honorary Professor, *Escuela Nacional de Ingenieros,* Lima, Peru

1954   Honorary Corresponding Member, League of Philippine Architects,
           Manila
           Socio Honorario, Instituto de Arquitetos do Brasil
           Establishment of Gropius Society in Tokyo, Japan
           Doctor of Science Degree (Honorary) conferred by the University of
           Sydney, Australia
           Socio Honorario, La Sociedad de Arquitectos del Peru
           Fellow of the American Institute of Architects
           Honorary Member and Silver Medal of Achievement, the Far East
           Society of Architects, Tokyo, Japan

1955   *Doutor Honoris Causa,* conferred by the University of Brazil, Rio de
           Janeiro

1956   Royal Gold Medal, the Royal Institute of British Architects, London
           Hanseatic Goethe Prize, awarded by the University of Hamburg, Ger-
           many

1957   Honorary Corresponding Member, *Accadèmia Nazionale di San Luca, Roma*
Honorary Member of the Deutscher Werkbund

1958   Honorary Member, *Accadèmia di Belle Arte di Venèzia*
The Grand Cross of Merit with Star, from the President of the Federal Republic of Germany

1959   Gold Medal of the American Institute of Architects

1960   Grand State Prize of Architecture, Germany

SELECTED BIBLIOGRAPHY OF BOOKS AND ARTICLES WRITTEN BY WALTER GROPIUS

BOOKS

Idee und Aufbau des Staatlichen Bauhauses, Weimar, Bauhausverlag GmbH., Munich, 1923.

Internationale Architektur, Bauhaus, Weimar, 1925.

Bauhausbauten Dessau, Bauhaus, Weimar, 1930.

The New Architecture and the Bauhaus, Faber and Faber, London, 1935; Museum of Modern Art, New York, 1936.

Bauhaus 1919-1928, edited by Herbert Bayer, Walter Gropius, Ise Gropius. Museum of Modern Art, New York, 1938. (German translation: Hatje, Stuttgart, 1955.)

Rebuilding Our Communities, Paul Theobald, Chicago, 1945.

Scope of Total Architecture, Harper, New York, 1955; Allen & Unwin, London, 1955. (Spanish translation: Ediciones La Isla, Buenos Aires, 1956; Japanese translation: Shokokusha, Tokyo, 1958; Italian translation: Mondadori, Milan, 1959.)

Architektur—Wege zu einer optischen Kultur (Buecher des Wissens), Fischer Buecherei, Frankfurt/Hamburg, 1956.

Arquitectura y Planeamiento, Ediciones Infinito, Buenos Aires, 1958.

ARTICLES

Programm zur Gründung einer Allgemeinen Hausbaugesellschaft auf künstlerisch einheitlicher Grundlage mbH. Ziel: Industrialisierung des Hausbaues. Manuscript, 1910.

"Die Entwicklung moderner Industriebaukunst," *Jahrbuch des Deutschen Werkbundes,* 1913.

"Das Manifest der neuen Architektur. Stein, Holz, Eisen," Frankfurt am Main, August 5, 1926.

"Offset-, Buch-, und Werbekunst," Sondernummer, Bauhaus-Heft no. 7, gesammelt von Moholy-Nagy (Beitrag von Gropius, Breuer, Moholy-Nagy, Albers, Bayer, Stoelzel, Schlemmer), Leipzig, 1926.

"Das flache Dach" (Umfrage, veranstaltet von W. Gropius), *Bauwelt,* Vol. 17, Berlin, 1926.

"Geistige und technische Voraussetzung der neuen Baukunst," *Umschau,* Vol. 31 (Frankfurt a.M.), 1927

F. Block, "Der Architekt als Organisator der modernen Bauwirtschaft und seine Forderungen an die Industrie," *Wohnbau,* Vol. 1, Müller & Kiepenheuer, Potsdam, 1928.

"Versuchssiedlung in Dessau," *Reichsforschungsgesellschaft für Wirtschaftlichkeit im Wohnungsbau,* Sonderheft 7, 1929.

"Der Gedanke der Rationalisierung in der Bauwirtschaft," *Deutsche Kunst und Dekoration,* Vol. 33, 1929.

"Grossiedlungen," *Zentralblatt der Bauverwaltung,* Berlin, March 26, 1930.

"Die soziologischen Grundlagen der Minimalwohnung für die städtische Industriebevölkerung," *Die Justiz,* Berlin, May, 1930.

"Die Wohnung für das Existenzminimum," *Internationale Kongresse für Neues Bauen (CIAM) und Städtisches Hochbauamt in Frankfurt am Main,* 1930.

"Flach-, Mittel-, oder Hochbau?" *Neues Frankfurt* (Frankfurt am Main), February, 1931.

"Wohnhochhäuser im Grünen. Eine grosstädtische Wohnform der Zukunft," *Zentralblatt der Bauverwaltung,* Heft 49/50, 1931.

"Arquitectura Funcional," *Arquitectura,* Madrid, Heft 2, 1931.

"Walter Gropius et la Jeune Ecole Allemande," *L'Architecture Vivante,* Morancé, Paris, 1932.

"Formal and Technical Problems of Modern Architecture and Planning," *Royal Institute of British Architects Journal,* Vol. 41, 1934.

"Theaterbau," *Reale Accadèmia d'Italia, Fondazione Alessandro Volta, Convegno di Lettere,* Rome, October, 1934.

"General Panel System," *Pencil Points,* April, 1943.

"Teaching the Arts of Design," *College Art Journal,* Vol. 7, No. 3, 1948.

"Organic Neighborhood Planning; Housing and Town and Country Planning," *Bulletin,* U.N., No. 2, April, 1949.

"Le Théâtre Total," *L'Architecture d'Aujourd'hui,* February, 1950. (With English translation.)

Speech at the 36th Annual Convention of the Association of Collegiate Schools of Architecture. *Association of Collegiate Schools of Architecture, Journal of Architectural Education,* No. 6, Spring, 1951.

"Faith in Planning (Planning, 1952)" (Proceedings of the Annual National Planning Conference), *American Society of Planning Officials,* October, 1952, Chicago, pp. 4-15.

"Wie sollen wir bauen (Die Baukunst ist keine angewandte Archäologie)," *Die neue Zeitung,* May, 1953.

"Apollo in der Demokratie," speech on occasion of the award of "Hansischer Goethe Preis," Hamburg, 1956, Gedenkschrift der gemeinnuetzigen Stiftung F.V.S. (English translation in *Zodiac,* No. 1, Milan, 1958.)

"Gestaltung von Museumsgebaeuden," *Jahresring 1955/1956,* Deutsche Verlagsanstalt, Stuttgart.

"The Curse of Conformity," *Saturday Evening Post,* June 6, 1958. (Reprinted in *Adventures of the Mind,* Knopf, 1959.)

"Architettura in Giapone," *Architettura: cantieri,* Milan, 1960.

SELECTED BIBLIOGRAPHY ON WALTER GROPIUS

BOOKS

Giedion, Sigfried, *Walter Gropius,* Crès & Cie, Paris, 1931.

Argan, G. C., *Walter Gropius e La Bauhaus,* Einaudi, Turin, 1951. (Spanish translation: Nueva Vision, Buenos Aires, 1957.)

Kurata, Chikatada, *Walter Gropius,* Tokyo, Japan, 1953.

Koyama, Masakazu, *Walter Gropius, Kokusai Kenchiku-Kyokai,* Shuppansha, Tokyo, 1954.

Yamawaki, Mityiko and Iwao, *Bauhaus Weimer-Dessau-Berlin,* Shokokusha, Tokyo, 1954.

The International House of Japan, *Gropius in Japan,* Tokyo, 1956.

Giedion, Sigfried, *Walter Gropius: Work and Teamwork,* published by M. E. Neuenschwander, Zurich, 1954 and issued simultaneously in English, French, German and Italian; in the United States by Reinhold, New York.

Herbert, Gilbert, *The Synthetic Vision of Walter Gropius,* Witwatersrand University Press, Johannesburg, South Africa, 1959.

Centro Estudiantes de Arquitectura, *Walter Gropius,* Montevideo, 1955.

ARTICLES AND REFERENCES IN BOOKS

"Die Faguswerke in Alfeld an der Leine," *Der Industriebau,* 1913.

"Die Werkbundausstellung in Köln a. Rh," *Jahrbuch des Deutschen Werkbundes,* 1915.

Wasmuth, Ernst, *Walter Gropius und Adolf Meyer, Bauten,* Berlin, 1923.

in Giedion, Sigfried, "Walter Gropius et l'Architecture en Allemagne," *Cahiers d'Art,* Vol. 5, 1930.

in Hitchcock, H.-R., *Modern Architecture,* Museum of Modern Art, New York, 1932.

in Hitchcock, H.-R. and Johnson, P. C., *International Style: Architecture since 1922,* Museum of Modern Art, New York, 1932.

in Sartoris, A., *Gli Elementi dell'Architettura Funzionale,* Hoepli, Milan, 1932.

in Pevsner, Nikolaus, *Pioneers of the Modern Movement from William Morris to Walter Gropius,* F. A. Stokes Co., New York, 1937; Museum of Modern Art, New York, 1947.

Perkins, G. H., "Walter Gropius," *Shelter,* April, 1938.

in Giedion, Sigfried, *Space, Time and Architecture,* Harvard University Press, Cambridge, 1941 (and subsequent editions).

in Sartoris, A., *Introduzione all'Architettura Moderna,* Hoepli, Milan, 1944.

in Zevi, Bruno, *Verso un'Architettura Organica,* Einaudi, Turin, 1945. (English translation: Faber and Faber, London.)

Martin, J. L., "The Bauhaus and its Influence," *Listener* (London), March 31, 1949.

"Walter Gropius et son Ecole," *L'Architecture d'Aujourd'hui,* February, 1950. (Special issue on Gropius.)

Shand, P. Morton, "The Bauhaus," *The Times Literary Supplement,* London, May 29, 1953.

Boyd, Robin, "Walter Gropius," Sydney (Australia) University Paper, August, 1954, in *Current Affairs Bulletin,* Vol. 14, No. 1.

in Fischer, Wend, *Die Kunst des 20. Jahrhunderts,* 3, R. Piper Verlag, Munich, 1957.

in Pevsner, Nikolaus, *Europaeische Architektur,* Prestel Verlag, Munich, 1957.

in Dorner, Alexander, *The Way Beyond Art,* New York University Press, New York, 1958.

in Rogers, Ernesto, *Esperienza dell'Architettura,* Einaudi, Turin, 1958.

in Ragon, Michel, *Le Livre de l'Architecture Moderne,* Robert Laffont, France, 1958.

in Joedicke, Jürgen, *Geschichte der Modernen Architektur,* Hatje, Stuttgart, 1959.

INDEX

Numbers in regular roman type refer to text pages; *italic* figures refer to the plates.

Academy of Philosophy, Erlangen (Gropius and Meyer), *14-16*

Adler: automobile, 16, *52, 53*

Albers, Anni, 16

Alfeld an der Leine, Germany: Fagus Factory (Gropius and Meyer), 18, 19-20, *1-3*

American Association for the Advancement of Science building, Washington, D.C. (Gropius and The Architects' Collaborative), *113*

American Institute of Architects: convention, New Orleans, 29; Gold Medal, 29

Architects' Collaborative, The, 25; *see also* Gropius and The Architects' Collaborative (partnership)

Art Nouveau, 19

Athens, Greece: United States Embassy (Gropius and The Architects' Collaborative), *118-21*

Austrian Pavilion, Cologne Werkbund Exhibition (Hoffman), 20

Automobile (Adler), 16, *52, 53*

Back Bay Center, Boston (Gropius and Boston Center Architects), *114-17*

Bagdad, Iraq: University of Bagdad (Gropius and The Architects' Collaborative), 9, 24-25, *124-35*

Ballet figures (Schlemmer), *34*

Bauhaus, the, 7-30 *passim;* buildings, Dessau, 21, 22, *17-27;* faculty housing, Dessau, 27, *40, 41;* style, 10-14, 17; *see also* Dessau and Weimar

Behrens, Peter, 8, 18, 19, 30; Berlin Turbine Factory, 19, *1a;* Exhibition Hall, Cologne Werkbund Exhibition, 20; German electrical trust, 8

Belluschi, Pietro; *see* Gropius, Emery Roth

Associates, and Pietro Belluschi (partnership)

Belmont, Massachusetts: Howlett house (Gropius and The Architects' Collaborative), *96, 97*

Berlage, H. P., 18

Berlin, Germany, 8, 26; gymnasium, Building Exhibition, *51;* Siemensstadt middle-class apartments, 26, *78-81;* standard furniture for Feder stores, *48, 49;* Total Theater, 21, 22-23, *54, 55, 57-61;* University of Charlottenburg, 8; Wannsee Slab Apartment Blocks, 26, *84-86*

Black Mountain College, Lake Eden, North Carolina (Gropius and Breuer), *103, 104*

Bogler, Theodore: porcelain ware, *32*

Boston, Massachusetts: Back Bay Center, *114-17*

Brandt, Marianne: metal utensils, *29, 33*

Brecht, Bertold, 22; *Three Penny Opera,* 22

Breuer, Marcel, 25, 26; tubular steel chair, 16, *30; see also* Gropius and Breuer (partnership)

Building Exhibition, Berlin: gymnasium, *51*

Cambridge, Massachusetts: *see* Harvard University

Cambridgeshire, England: Impington College buildings (Gropius and Fry), 24, *88-90*

Chamberlain house, Sudbury (Gropius and Breuer), *95*

Chapel, Ronchamp (Le Corbusier), 25

Chicago, Illinois, 13; McCormick office building (Gropius and The Architects' Collaborative), *112;* Tribune Tower competition entry (Gropius and Meyer), 16, 21-22, *11*

Chicago School (style), 19
Cologne, Germany: Werkbund Exhibition, 18, 20
Constructivist painting, 15
Cubism, 30

Dessau, Germany: the Bauhaus, 12, 14, 28; Bauhaus buildings, 21, 22, 27, *17-27, 40, 41;* Municipal Employment Office, *44-47;* Toerten housing, 26, 27, *70-72*
Diesel locomotive, 21, *4*
Doesburg, Theo van, 30

Eclecticism, 14, 16, 18, 20, 22
Einstein, Albert, 7, 30
Eleven Story Slab Apartment Block, *82, 83*
Engineering School, Hagen, Westphalia: entry for competition, *87*
Erlangen, Germany: Academy of Philosophy, *14-16*
Exhibition Hall, Cologne Werkbund Exhibition (Behrens), 20

Fabric, hand-woven (Willers), *28*
Faculty housing, Bauhaus; *see* Bauhaus
Fagus factory, Alfeld an der Leine (Gropius and Meyer), 18, 19-20, *1-3*
Feder stores, Berlin: standard furniture, *48, 49*
Feininger, Lyonel, 26, 30, *17*
Frank, Ise, 23
Fry, Maxwell, 24, 25; *see also* Gropius and Fry (partnership)
"Functional Style," 13
Furniture: for Feder stores, *48, 49;* ceiling lamp, *31;* steel, for battleship, 21; luxury, for villa, 21

Garnier, Charles, 24; Paris Opera House, 23, *56*
Gaudí, Antonio, 18, 19
General Panel Corporation prefabricated house, 27
German electrical trust (Behrens), 8
German Werkbund Exhibition, Paris: hall and bar, *50*
Giedion, Sigfried, 20, 30
Grand Central City Building, New York (Gropius, Emery Roth Associates, and Pietro Belluschi), *136-38*
Grand Ducal Academy of Arts, 11, 21

Grand Ducal School of Applied Arts, 11, 21
Grand Duke of Saxe-Weimar, 21
Gropius, Alma Mahler, 20-21, 26
Gropius, Ise Frank, 23
Gropius, Manon (mother), 8
Gropius, Walter (father), 8
Gropius and The Architects' Collaborative (partnership) 25; American Association for the Advancement of Science building, *113;* Harvard Graduate Center, 24, *105-11;* Howlett house, *96, 97;* McCormick office building, *112;* Rudow-Bukow housing development, *122, 123;* United States Embassy, Athens, *118-21;* University of Bagdad, 9, 24-25, *124-35*
Gropius and Boston Center Architects (associated) Back Bay Center, *114-17*
Gropius and Breuer (partnership), 25; Black Mountain College, *103, 104;* Chamberlain house, *95;* Gropius house, Lincoln, 24, *91-94;* New Kensington housing project, 24, *98-102*
Gropius and Fry (partnership), 24, 25; Impington College buildings, 24, *88-90*
Gropius and Meyer (partnership), 25; Academy of Philosophy, *14-16;* Fagus Factory, 18, 19-20, *1-3;* municipal theater, Jena (remodeled), 22; office building, pavilion for Deutz Factory, Cologne Werkbund Exhibition, 20, *6-10;* Tribune Tower competition entry, 16, 21-22, *11*
Gropius, Emery Roth Associates, and Pietro Belluschi (partnership): Grand Central City Building, *136-38*
Gropius residences: Dessau, *35-39;* Lincoln, Massachusetts (Gropius and Breuer), 24, *91-94*
Guggenheim Museum, New York City (Wright), 25

Hagen, Germany: design for Engineering School, *87*
Halle, Germany: Theater, 22
Harvard University, Cambridge, 8, 12; Graduate Center (Gropius and The Architects' Collaborative), 24, *105-11;* Graduate School of Design, 12, 26
Hauptmann, Gerhart, 30
Hitchcock, Henry-Russell, 16
Hitler, Adolf, 14, 23, 28, 29

Hoffman, Joseph, 18; Austrian Pavilion, 20
Horta, Victor, 18
Howells and Hood (partnership): Tribune Tower competition winning entry, 22, *13*
Howlett house, Belmont (Gropius and The Architects' Collaborative), *96, 97*

Impington College buildings, Cambridgeshire (Gropius and Fry), 24, *88-90*
"International Style," 13
International theater conference, Rome, 23-24
Itten, Johannes, 26

Japanese architecture, 30-31
Jeanneret, Charles; *see* Le Corbusier
Jefferson, Thomas, 22
Jena, Germany: Municipal Theater (Gropius and Meyer), 22
Jugendstil, 18

Kandinsky, Wassily, 26, 30
Kharkov, U.S.S.R.: Ukrainian State Theater, 22, *62, 63*
Klee, Paul, 16, 26, 30
Kokoschka, 30

Larkin Building (Wright), 19, *1b*
Le Corbusier, 8, 16, 25, 28; chapel, Ronchamp, 25
Lincoln, Massachusetts: Gropius house (Gropius and Breuer), 24, *91-94*
London, England, 8, 23
Loos, Adolf, 14, 18; *Ornament and Crime*, 14; Doric column for Tribune Tower competition, 22, *12*

MacIntosh, Charles Rennie, 18
McCormick Office Building, Chicago (Gropius and The Architects' Collaborative), *112*
Mahler, Alma, 20-21, 26
Malevich, Kazimir S., 30
Marxism, 29
Matisse, Henri, 7
Mendelsohn, Eric, 26
Meyer, Adolph, 22, 25; *see also* Gropius and Meyer (partnership)
Mies (van der Rohe), Ludwig, 8, 25, 28, 30; Seagram building, 25

Model factory, Cologne Werkbund Exhibition; *see* pavilion for Deutz Factory, Cologne Werkbund Exhibition
Modernismo, 19
Moholy-Nagy, L., 15, 26, 30
Moholy-Nagy house, *42-43*
Mondrian, P. C., 30
Moscow, U.S.S.R.: Palace of the Soviets, theater, 22, *64-69*
Munich, Germany: University of Munich, 8
Municipal Employment Office, Dessau, *44-47*
Municipal Theater, Jena (Gropius and Meyer), 22

Nagel, Chester, 26
Neumann, J. B., 26
New Kensington housing project, Pittsburgh, (Gropius and Breuer), 24, *98-102*
New Orleans, Louisiana, 29; American Institute of Architects Convention, 29
New York City: Grand Central City building (Gropius, Emery Roth Associates, and Pietro Belluschi), *136-38*
Non-Objectivism, 30
North Carolina: Black Mountain College, *103, 104*

Opera House, Paris (Garnier), 23, *56*
Ornament and Crime (Loos), 14

Palace of the Soviets, Moscow: Theater, 22, *64-69*
Palladio, Andrea: *Teatro Olimpico*, 23
Pavilion for Deutz Factory, Cologne Werkbund Exhibition (Gropius and Meyer), 20, *6-10*
Piscator, Erwin, 22
Pittsburgh, Pennsylvania: New Kensington housing project (Gropius and Breuer), 24, *98-102*
Poelzig, Hans, 30
Porcelain ware (Bogler), *32*
Prairie houses (Wright), 18
Prefabricated copper houses, *74-77*
Prefabricated house, Werkbund Housing Exhibition, 27

Reinhardt, Max, 30
Rome, Italy, 23; international theater conference, 23-24

Roth, Emery; see Gropius, Emery Roth Associates, and Pietro Belluschi (partnership)   ;
Rudow-Bukow housing development, West Berlin (Gropius and The Architects' Collaborative), *122, 123*

Saturday Evening Post, The, 28-29
Schlemmer, Oscar, 22, 30; *Triadic Ballet,* 22; ballet figures, *34*
Schlesinger-Meyer Store (Sullivan), 19, *1c*
Schönberg, Arnold, 30
Seagram building, New York City (Mies), 25
Secessionstil, 19
Shaw, George Bernard, 7
Siemensstadt apartments, Berlin, 26, *78-81*
Sleeping car for the German Railway, Cologne Werkbund Exhibition, 21, *5*
Spain, 8
Sturm, Der, 15
Stuttgart, Germany: Weissenhof prefabricated house, Werkbund Exhibition, *73*
Sudbury, Massachusetts: Chamberlain house, *95*
Sudermann, Hermann, 30
Sullivan, Louis, 8, 18; Schlesinger-Meyer Store, 19, *1c*

Taliesin, Wisconsin (Wright), 25
Teatro Olimpico (Palladio), 23
Theater, Cologne Werkbund Exhibition (van de Velde), 20
Theater, Halle, 22
Three Penny Opera (Brecht and Weill), 22
Toerten Housing, Dessau, 26, 27; model of construction sequence, *70;* row houses, *71, 72*
Total Theater, Berlin, 22, 22-23, *54, 55, 57-61*
Triadic Ballet (Schlemmer), 22
Tribune Tower, Chicago, international competition for, 21-22; Gropius and Meyer entry, 16, 21-22, *11;* Howells and Hood entry, 22, *13;* Loos entry, 22, *12*
Turbine Factory, Berlin (Behrens), 19, *1a*

Ukrainian State Theater, Kharkov, 22, *62, 63*
United States Embassy, Athens (Gropius and The Architects' Collaborative), *118-21*
Unity Temple (Wright), 19
University of Bagdad, Iraq (Gropius and The Architects' Collaborative), 9, 24-25, *124-35*
University of Charlottenburg, Berlin, 8
University of Munich, 8
Utensils, metal (Brandt), *29, 33*
Utopia, 29

Velde, Henry van de, 18, 21; Theater, Cologne Werkbund Exhibition, 20
Voysey, C. F. A., 18

Wagner, Otto, 18
Wannsee Slab Apartment Blocks, Berlin, 26, *84-86*
Washington, D.C.: American Association for the Advancement of Science building, *113*
Weill, Kurt, 22; *Three Penny Opera,* 22
Weimar, Germany: Bauhaus, 11, 12, 14, 18, 21, 22, 28, 29
Weimar Staatliches Bauhaus, 11, 21; *see also* Bauhaus
Weissenhof prefabricated house, Werkbund Exhibition, Stuttgart, *73*
Werfel, Franz, 30
Werkbund Exhibition, Cologne, 18, 20; Austrian Pavilion (Hoffman), 20; Exhibition Hall (Behrens), 20; office building, pavilion for Deutz Factory (Gropius and Meyer), 20, *6-10;* sleeping car, 21, *5;* Theater (van de Velde), 20; yearbooks of, 21
Werkbund Housing Exhibition, 27
West Berlin, Germany: Rudow-Bukow housing development (Gropius and The Architects' Collaborative), *122, 123*
Willers, Margarete: hand-woven fabric, *28*
Wright, Frank Lloyd, 7, 18, 19, 25, 28; Guggenheim Museum, 25; Larkin building, 19, *1b;* Prairie houses, 19; Taliesin, 25; Unity Temple, 19

SOURCES OF ILLUSTRATIONS

Bauhaus, Dessau: 69
Bautechniche Mitteilungen, July, 1914: 9
Berliner-Bild-Bericht, Berlin: 50
Cousenmiller, Bauhaus, Dessau: 23, 24, 70
Robert Damora, New Canaan, Connecticut: 91, 93, 94
Davis Studio, Boston: 103
Dell and Wainwright, *Architectural Review:* 88, 89
Hermann Eckner, Weimar: 14
Feder, *Katalog des Warenhauses,* 1930: 49
Lyonel Feininger, Bauhaus, Dessau: 17
Walter R. Fleischer, Cambridge: 109, 110
Gottscho-Schleisner, New York: 98, 101, 102
Walter Gropius: 2, 4, 55, 58
Harvey Studio, Boston: 112, 113, 114, 115, 116, 117, 119, 122, 126
Arthur Köster, Berlin: 74, 75, 76, 78, 80, 81
André LeJeune and Stéphane Wolff, *Les Quinze Salles de L'Opéra de Paris 1669-1955,* Libraire
    Théatrale, Paris, 1955: 56
Leonard, Berlin: 19
Lossen, Stuttgart: 73
Lucia Moholy-Nagy, Dessau: 18, 30, 36, 37, 38, 40, 41, 42
Peterhans, Bauhaus, Dessau: 25
Photo-Illustration, Paris: 34
Photothen, Berlin, 21
John Pimlott, New York: 138
Renger-Photo, D.W.B.: 1, 3
Ezra Stoller, Rye, New York: 95, 96, 97
Fred Stone, Cambridge: 105, 108, 111
Theiss, Dessau: 44, 72
The Tribune Tower Competition, Chicago Tribune Company, Chicago, 1923: 11, 12, 13
Van der Ziepen und Charlier GmbH.: 5